A Trip Down th

C000227100

With Best
Wishes

Gary Smith

FOREWORD

The shopping roads of Brum once cut through each and every working-class neighbourhood. They were packed with a variety of retailers, they pounded with the feet of keen shoppers and they resounded with the cries of street traders and characters. They were atmospheric, they were bustling and they were essential. Essential because each one was an artery for its working-class locality, drawing folk to it and by so doing bringing together all of the loosely-defined and merging urban villages which lay off it. Just think of all those wonderful shopping thoroughfares: Great Lister Street for Duddeston; Nechells Park Road for Nechells, Down the Rock (the Alum Rock Road) for Saltley and Alum Rock; Up the Cov (the Coventry Road) for Small Heath and Hay Mills; On the Bend at Gooch Street for Highgate; Down the Lane (the Ladypool Road) for Sparkbrook; Up the Mo (the Moseley Road) for Balsall Heath; Cregoe Street for the Holloway Head and Bath Row areas; Aston Cross and High Street Aston; Up the Main (the Soho Road) for Handsworth; Gosta Green; Deritend High Street; the Stratford Road for Sparkhill and Springfield; the Warwick Road at Greet; Spring Hill; Monument Road for Ladywood; and the Bristol Road for Bournbrook and Selly Oak. And then there were all the village centres such as Kings Heath, Northfield, Erdington, Moseley, Ward End, Harborne and others.

Each shopping thoroughfare had certain shops in common with others - like Wrenson's, Masons's, the Maypole and the like - but each also boasted its own particular traders. And that's how it was on 'The Flat' - one of the greatest of the shopping roads of Old Brum. Serving folk of Hockley, Brookfields, Gib Heath and Winson Green, it also pulled in Brummies from further afield. Destroyed by the redevelopments which swept across post-war Birmingham, The Flat is little more than a memory. That is why Gary Smith's book is so important. It brings to the fore both the vitality and importance of The Flat. 'A Trip Down the Flat is a tribute to all the traders and shoppers who made The Flat one of the best-known and most significant of the shopping centres of working-class Brummagem.

A TRIP DOWN

Gary Smith

THE FLAT

BREWIN
BOOKS

First Published by Brewin Books Ltd
Studley, Warwickshire. B80 7LG
in December 2000

© Gary Smith 2000
All rights reserved.

The author's moral right has been asserted.

British Library Cataloguing In Publication Data.
A Catalogue record for this book is available
from The British Library

ISBN 1 85858 180 X

Typeset in Palatino.
Made and printed in Great Britain by
SupaPrint (Redditch) Ltd.
Redditch, Worcestershire.
Website: www.supaprint.com
E-mail: admin@supaprint.com

DEDICATION

I would like to have dedicated this book to our mom once again, but unfortunately she died a few months before it was finished, but no matter, it will be posthumous for her and for our dad. Without them naturally I wouldn't be here, but this is also for my family, I want my grandchildren to understand what it was like for their grandma and grandad to grow up in another age.

BY THE SAME AUTHOR

Winson Green - My World   Brewin Books

A Walk Up The Green   Brewin Books

ACKNOWLEDGEMENTS

As in my previous books, I should like to thank all of the people who helped me in my quest to write the last remaining sequel to our area, Johnny Landon for his photo's, as well as Ted Rudge, Ray Clarke, Barbara Boscott, Hilda Fry, Vic Jones and all the rest, if I've missed anyone out I apologise, but no doubt they will find themselves somewhere in this book. To Carl Chinn for his help, and Ron 'Smudge' Smith for his colour illustration, without all of these I wouldn't have been able to start it, don't know about finishing, but most of all to you for finding faith in me in writing about our area. There is one soul mate though, and that's our 'Marg', she's helped all along with these books and without her inspiration I couldn't have done them. Thank you all, and please read on.

CONTENTS

INTRODUCTION

A TRIP DOWN THE FLAT

This is the third and last part of my tour around Winson Green. From a small settlement around the Hockley Brook in the 13th century and to the re-spelling of our area many times, it became the area that we know of today. Staffordshire and Warwickshire were to meet and create yet another extension from the old town. We weren't to understand all of this as progress swept away any historical meaning to the area. Our area was special as it contained a wealth of industrial and social history. As I've said on a number of occasions, we weren't to realise it was to be just another homogeneous part of the tapestry of Birmingham. It would be hard to visualise the area from the first settlement to the present. This I hope will counter all the thoughts of Winson Green as just being home for a prison, asylum and workhouse. It was more. I hope that I have done our part of the city a service, up to the present we have made our journey from Springhill to the borders with Edgbaston and Smethwick. Now we are on our last part of our journey in our district.

Those of us who came from Winson Green would have at one time or another made a trip on the 96 bus or the 32 tram to a renowned shopping area called the "Flat". This area was at the bottom of Lodge Rd. The journey itself started from the bottom of Foundry Rd. It continued down Lodge Rd past the mental hospital, climbing up the hill pass Tynegates wood yard. Even though now we came into Brookfields we still classed this area an extension to Winson Green. Getting off the bus at the Hydraulic public house in All Saints Rd we would make our way round the corner opposite Scribbans' bakery down the steep hill (well it seemed like it at the time) and to a cornucopia of shops.

This is the start of my story which will involve others along the way. On that short trip from the border with Smethwick to Hockley none of us realised what history we had passed, including the mental hospital which was known as Birmingham Asylum, built in 1851 on heathland with the prison and the workhouse. Slowly houses began to fill in the area between the asylum and Handsworth. Soho Pool was filled in, and houses were compressed between Park Rd and Lodge Rd. This is the last part to the story on Winson Green. The area wasn't just a road that made its way from

Edgbaston to Handsworth. It had its own wealth of history and sense of purpose in the make up of Birmingham. We've made our way around the top of the Green with the building-up of the area. All the way down Wellington St to the Black Patch park. Now we come to the point of this next story.

We finished in the previous book at a focal point at the bottom of Winson Green Rd with Dolman's garage. This is now where we shall start on our new journey. I was only a lad but that trip made a lasting impression on me. At the top of Foundry Rd we came into Handsworth New Rd.and then the trip to the 'Flat' really began. It was then that Lodge Rd, Bacchus Rd and all of the streets that went off it made up this area. The people, the shops and workplaces of this last bastion of Winson Green. This now is the starting point to this story. I have called this book a "Trip Down The Flat" for a purpose. To a majority of us who lived at the bottom of the Green this was our route into the city centre, the "Flat" was the half way stage. This was a focal shopping area for the people from the roads and streets around Lodge Rd.

This artery from Winson Green Rd to the "Town" holds a wealth of history, let us find out more of the building up and development of the area.

"Move along the bus please, next stop the Flat".

THE 96 BUS TO ANOTHER WORLD

I remember the trams, but only vaguely. Like a majority of kids of our time, to go outside of one particular area would be an adventure, unlike today, to ride on a tram was an adventure. I would have only been about four when eventually buses took over this route into the town. The most outstanding part (and everlasting) was when the tram went round the sharp right hand bend by the mental hospital and Bacchus Rd and down the short steep hill to the Devonshire pub. It seemed to me that the tram would topple over, but that was only just a memory to me. This route was the 32, when buses took over from the tram it was renamed the 96.

My trip (or as best I can remember) to the 'Flat' started from outside the Railway Inn on the corner of Wellington St and Vittoria St. This was the terminus. The tram would run down Foundry Rd into Vittoria St towards the railway viaduct, change over tracks and run back up to the pub, where it would start it journey back to the town. I just remember this but later on when the buses took over, instead of going straight down Foundry Rd the bus turned into Franklin St then into Wellington St and then on to the terminus under the railway bridge, (handy for when it was pouring with rain). The 'Bundy' clock was brought from over the road from outside the Railway Inn under the bridge. One thing which I remember was that all the kids would wait till the driver was ready to depart, after which he would clock on and we would put out the backs of our hands for him to impress the key on our skin. The key had the driver's own number on it and would transfer the indelible ink on our skin, happy days. Whilst I vaguely remember the trams, the bus journey has always stayed in my memory.

My journey was to make it's way up Foundry Rd., past my old school, Foundry Rd, and the cobblers on the corner of James Turner St past Mrs Clayburns who kept a sweet shop, who I remember sold liquorice root, all for a penny a strip, we would suck it till their was no juice left in it, just a soggy piece of wood! This was another little shopping centre as all districts had. The bus then turned into Handsworth New Rd at the junction of Winson Green Rd and into Lodge Rd. The first stop was outside Bannister and Thatchers the chemist's, past our old doctor's surgery, Dr Mackiernan. On the right were the prison warders houses standing under

The 32 Tram outside the Railway Pub in Vittoria Street
at the terminus prior to 1947
(Author)

The 96 bus outside Foundry Road Schools
much much later on
(Author)

the high walls of the prison. The prison walls ended as the walls of the mental hospital took over, it seemed where ever we looked around the Green we looked at high walls. On the left hand side lay Victor Rd abutting onto the walls of Bushells the ex-army surplus site, the large house and grounds were to be developed and a new road in Winson Green was to built and known as Rectory Grove (normally groves were used as grand sounding names for back houses, but this one was for a real street). Next door came the Golden Eagle pub, a few houses and a garage and past Bacchus Rd, with the public washing baths on the left just inside the road.

The start of the journey, Foundry Road, before re-development.
(A Dolman)

Round the sharp right hand bend past the Don public house and Don St and Talbot St then past the entrance on the right to the Mental Hospital, and finally down the remainder of the hill to the Devonshire Arms on the corner of Musgrave Rd and Devonshire St, past Lodge Rd Congregational Church and Lees St, then the steady climb up the hill past Kent St North and Norton St. The bus stop was right outside one of my old mates Gary Margetts. The bus was now full and it struggled till it reached the top of hill to the canal. This was now Brookfields, we were now officially out of Winson Green but in mind only. Over the railway bridge and Abbey St.

3

The beginning of Lodge Road in the 1970s not much altered
apart from the removal of houses on the right
(A Dolman)

Here the connotations of a religious theme would stick in my mind, we shall find out later on in the book this was to be more of fiction than of fact. The bus then turned into All Saints St opposite one of the oldest bread firms in the area by the name of Scribbans'. Mothers, kids in arms and younger ones at their side and the rest of the shoppers would then alight and make their remaining walk down Lodge Rd to the 'Flat'. Then after an hour or so would make their way back up the hill bags in hand for the return journey.

That was it really . Not really that earth shattering, but to a young lad who lived on the Staffordshire borders, this was a travelling experience. It of course led onto a much larger vista, we knew after the 'Flat' there would be the town. The hustle and bustle of a great city, but on this day it was to be the 'Flat' and for the weekly shop at George Mason's and the rest. Everything that our mom would need was there to be had from that shopping area. It's now just a distant memory, but I'll never forget it.
We need now to go back a few hundred yards or more, and find out about the last part of our story of Winson Green. We never realised that from

4

humble beginnings from the massive walls of the Mental Asylum over to the area of the Soho Pool, this was to be another area that was to be packed with typical working class dwellings with it's own corner shops, pub's and, most of all, its people. Roads and streets were to change names over the following many years. We grew up with the latter names on their respective street corners, flashing past as we made our way to the 'Flat'. It was another part, as far as we were concerned, of Winson Green. Another greater extension to my area. It was to be other people's memories of a period in their lives. Their schools, places of work, recreation, and for the more religious, their places of worship. Another piece of the patchwork quilt of the people who made up this corner of Winson Green.

That was my journey to the 'Flat'. Along the way it was to be a longer journey for others who were to make this their homes, Let us find out more about the beginning and the history which made up this part of Birmingham.

Rectory Grove, Victor Road behind built on Bushels
the Ex. Army War Surplus Business
(J Landon)

Looking down Lodge Road in the 1950s Don Street on the left.
(J Landon)

The Devonshire Arms (still there today)
Not so much of the property around
(J Landon)

Congregational Church, Lodge Road, home to many organisations
(J Landon)

THE WAY TO THE NINEVAH

It almost sounds like a passage from a thousand and one nights. This is now where our story enfolds. The road out of the old town of Birmingham to the North west would have made its way to Snow Hill, then up Constitution Hill and into Great Hampton St. and onwards to the Wednesbury Rd. This was one of the two toll roads out of Birmingham to the West, the other being the Dudley Rd. At the rise of the hill before crossing the Hockley Brook a road went offto the left, this was Key Hill. It wan't always known as this for in the early 18th century a farmer by the name of J Tookey owned the land and the hill was known as Tookeys Hill. This name stuck till it was renamed Key Hill in the 1800's, and then met the junction with Icknield St.

Cottages at rear of Key Hill in the 1950s.
Possibly on the site of Tookeys Farm from the 18th century.
(J Landon)

Up until 1840 much of Birmingham to the West was pretty well undeveloped. It was as if an invisible barrier stopped Birmingham from building after Icknield St. The town was growing more crowded from the centre, and the only way for it to expand was to the west. It was provident that there was a vast expanse of heath to develop on. In this respect it was fortunate that this area was owned by prominent Birmingham landowners.

Wealthy people who had moved from the centre of the town, and resided where now stands the Jewellery Quarter were slowly being taken over by small factories. For the more affluent the need to move was even more paramount. Estates later on in the century were built on the outskirts of Birmingham for the more prosperous folks of our city, such as Edgbaston, notably the Calthorpe Estate. Other areas attracted a want for less polluted air notably Erdington and Sutton Coldfield. But that is not where we are going, as we are stopping in our area.

Cheney's Factory close to the site of Boulton's Manufactory.
(D Avery)

Land was available closer at home and our new entrepreneurs in business would want to live nearer to their factories. Matthew Boulton was one such man. After leaving Snow Hill he resided at Soho House overlooking his new factory. We know why the land was developed between the town and Smethwick in the West. The opening up of the heath wasn't developed all into one big building plot at the same time. Areas were still available for the more well off. Boundaries as yet hadn't been as hard defined as now. Handsworth Heath was still very rural and wealthy people would have had their houses built there, including James Watt. Watt's address was Heathfield House in 1790, possibly close to what is now Heathfield Rd. Murdoch the remaining part of the trio had his house house built at Sycamore Hill and was naturally named the Sycamores, in the area which was called the Ninevah. After their deaths the houses were lived in for a number of years. Eventually they were pulled down, Watt's in 1927, and Murdoch's curiously the same year. Only Boulton's house still stands today. (Still I suppose on Birmingham's record one out of three to be still around for the history books isn't so bad!) It must have looked impressive. It overlooked the Great Pool. The Hockley Brook that made it's way from out of Staffordshire entered the lake and then made it's way through Hockley eventually going into the River Rea.

Coming out of the town down Key Hill and across Icknield St the ground flattened out before rising up again, this is now what we called the 'Flat'. In later years it was to be called Lodge Rd . This wasn't always the case . The first name I can find was called Grosvenor Place, then Hockley Pool Rd. At the split of the road the ground began to rise, the one way was up Lodge Rd and the other Park Rd. Even these weren't the original names. Park Rd was called Lodge Rd!

From Grosvenor Place to Boulton's estate stood Hockley Abbey, not a religious building but not unlike one. The 'Abbey' was a gothic folly, built by a Richard Ford in 1779 and built of 'coal slag!'. It's facade was decorated with pebbles and he grew ivy over it to make it look like a medieval ruin. He even added a plaque claiming it had been built in 1473! He was an eccentric as well as a teetotaller and claimed to have built the folly on the amount of money his workers had spent on beer, which he amounted to two shillings a day, his name was to be for posterity in that they named a street after him. After the building up of the area, the 'Abbey' was demolished and only the name Abbey St has any reminder of this folly.

Not only houses, pubs and places of work were to be built, the spiritual part of the district was to follow. An Anglican church was built, this was to be All Saints, just around the corner from Abbey St. The other were the

Catholic equivalents, St Francis in Hockley and St Patricks on the Dudley Rd, other Anglican churches followed with St Cuthberts in Winson Green Rd and Bishop Latimers in Handsworth New Rd, though this one wasn't built till the turn of the century. In between this time non conformist churches sprang up rapidly in our area, but we'll get back to them later on.

On the way to Handsworth in Staffordshire the lane which led to the Boulton's estate and manufactory was to be called Lodge Rd, The reason for this seemed plausible, as it would have led to the lodge entrance to the estate. It must have looked impressive. It would have opened onto the vista of the Great Pool, and beyond a smaller pool known as the Shell Pool. So clean were the waters that it is documented that a Salmon was caught from Hockley Brook at this time. The estate would have seemed even more impressive from Boulton's house which overlooked the scene from Soho Avenue. The road continued after this to an area called the Ninevah, which was on Handsworth Heath and we find the early map writers would call this road the way to the Ninevah. Over the years the name changed to Park Rd. Why it did? I can't understand. As there wasn't a park, and the pool was filled in before the name changed.

When the London and North Western Railway built the Soho Loop line from north of Perry Barr, through Handsworth and then into Birmingham, the pool had been drained and was then developed into a goods yard. The original line from Perry Barr wasn't opened till 1887, and the first tracks were laid to Handsworth Pool (Soho Pool). The two pools were drained and culverted. There was no way that the pools could have been kept open in parkland as the brook coming from out of Staffordshire was getting more polluted through heavy industry as the years went by. By now there were two railway companies alongside each other. The Great Western from Wolverhampton, and the predecessors to the L M S from the main line at Perry Barr. Within the space of 40 years the railways had taken over from the more sedate canal system. With the Hockley Pool depot and Hockley goods yard at All Saints the area changed out of all recognition. The original Soho Manufactory was pulled down in the 1800's and the only building still standing is Boulton's house in Soho Avenue. Now we can go on to the forming of Lodge Rd and the way to Winson Green.

Lodge road down to the 'flat' was to fill in with roads, streets and houses from the newly built asylum to Park Rd. Like the 'Way to the Ninevah', this was the way to Winson Green. After this the road climbs up till crossing the arm off the old canal which was excavated in the 1700's. This little arm made its way towards a wharf, why was it built? It wasn't to service Boulton's new manufactory, as the canal is shown on a map of 1731 and the Soho Works weren't in operation till the 1760's. Some historians on Birmingham believe this arm was to service the above. Perhaps the cartographer of the time hadn't yet updated his map!

Later on small factories and coal yards would run alongside the canal down to the wharf. On the other side of Lodge Rd stood the old fever hospital which has since been pulled down. This was away from the main buildings which formed the workhouse and infirmary. After this came Birmingham's Lunatic Asylum and a continuous wall apart from the entrance to the asylum in Lodge Rd, and the prison gates in Winson Green Rd would continue up the Green and back along the canal towards the workhouse. Where ever we stood in our area there was always a high wall for something or another!

The asylum was built in 1850 at around the time of the new Borough Gaol. It was designed by D.R.Hill who also instrumental in the design of the prison. Up to this time there was another asylum in the town, it was situated at the bottom of Summer Lane towards Lozells, this would eventually close down and the patients would have been moved to Winson Green. It was purpose built and stood in its own grounds, almost park like, it even had its own area set aside for vegetable growing, and was pretty well self sufficient. These institutions and the factories around would need to be serviced by labour and so the streets and houses would take shape and be filled once again by an influx of people from the surrounding shires.

In 1857 according to one map there were only nine streets off the Lodge Rd from Norton St to the Bacchus Rd and down to Park Rd. Within ten years this would have more than doubled, and by the turn of the century it was to be three times the amount, so we can see how the need for more housing was to be paramount. In the 1850's the open countryside from the bottom end of Lodge Rd to the area known as the Ninevah was slowly being devoured by the incoming population and their need for accommodation. In between Bacchus Rd and the border with Staffordshire (by the Black Patch Park) there was only one road, and that was Handsworth New Rd, not another street or road was there to be seen in the 1850's. The land was the remainder of Birmingham Heath, odd smallholdings dotted about here and there. Apart from James Turner's house which I have previously written about, the land was mostly open and unused.

All Saints Hospital, Lodge Road, Winson Green
Birmingham Borough Lunatic Asylum built 1847 - 1850
(T Rudge)

In 1855 from a street map by L. Piggot Smith of the borough of Birmingham, the layout of the roads didn't vary much from today. Only they were named differently. Such as Lodge Rd (which was called Winson Green Rd!). Coming over the canal at the rise of the hill, the first road was, and is, Norton St followed by Foster St (where Lees St stood), before being called Devonshire St was Napier St which came next, off this street was Baltic St, and a bit further along Lodge Rd lay Raglan St, a little bit further on was Musgrave St, in between the last two was Alma St. We know that some of these street names were not really adopted, but the question arises were they ever used? we'll never know.

All of these streets ran directly to Park Rd which was known then as Lower Lane. There were no other streets till Bacchus Rd, even then it was called a lane, which ran into Soho Rd (Benson Rd) and carried on till it ran into Factory Lane (Road) and went down to Boulton's manufactory. Within a couple of years though others streets were to be built such as Don, Talbot, Kent St Nth, Radnor and Dover St.

One of the original streets to have kept its name was Wharf St which ran down from the basin of the canal into Park Rd. This would have been the way to and from the Manufactory for transportation.

At the bottom of Lodge Rd the land at this point was at its lowest, and lo and behold there was another pool which occupied an area where Musgrave Rd and Devonshire St now stand, and that was Meredith's pool. The area must have been a cornucopia for the budding fisherman at that time! but like all the rest it was to be filled in, and the inevitable ribbon of houses were continuing to be built.

Let's now return to the top of Lodge Rd for a moment. Tynegates timber yard we all remember, and next to that was a building owned by Ford's the motor manufacturer. This was a testing bed for some of the well known cars in the 60's. Vic Hickinbottom from up the Green worked there in the 1950's and remembers the design and mock up of the latest Ford Anglia, which was to make it's appearance in 1960. This was Ford's answer to the successful Mini, which came out 12 months earlier. Even the Green had it's latter day celebrities which we didn't know about.

What we didn't realise though was that this building was one of the first glasshouses on the Green, owned by a Mr Shakespeare (no relation to the famous one) in 1740. After that it was the Vesta and Soho Glassworks, and continued as a glassworks till after the last war, though not with the same name.

This was to be the furthest that Birmingham would stretch. Handsworth wouldn't come into the fold till the early 20th century! When eventually Birmingham was to be made a city. Handsworth Heath ran naturally into Birmingham Heath, but it was still separate from Birmingham as a whole, and Murdoch travelled back into Staffordshire to his country retreat.
We now know of the make up and the history to this part of Winson Green, of where and when we made our route out of the city, our local history and how we made our mark on the world, but let's find out about the real people that made up the area. We need now to go into the 20th century and meet our neighbours.

FROM BOURNEMOUTH TO BRUM

It was to be a bit of a mix and match. The Boulters who came from Bournemouth were from Wales originally then came to live in Birmingham. It was to be a culture shock, to come from a lovely part of Dorset to a great and bustling city such as Brum, even more so with the reputation Winson Green had. It had developed and grown with the building of a prison, workhouse and an asylum. Life and times were hard, more so for Sheila's mother. After coming up to Birmingham the Boulter children were put in St Francis's Convent in Hockley, which was to be their home till they were old enough to go out to work, her parents had to pay for the schooling. Life in those days was hard at the convent. Even though they were well cared for, the nuns were very strict, and really there wasn't that much love shown. Attitudes only changed when payments were made to the convent at the beginning of the term, but soon went back to normal after a short time. Sheila had a good mother and was brought up as well as any in Talbot St, but there was something missing, and as Sheila grew up she understood why. Their mother had been brought up in a strict regime and that little bit of love had been taken away from her.

Years later her mother was to meet her father and her name changed to Clemens, he came from the Green. He was one of a large family, and would have been larger, had it not been for poor sanitation, housing and of course a right diet. T.B. would take a large toll on his family. After getting married they settled in Norman St and later on were able to make an exchange to 4 back of 90 Talbot St where three girls and a lad were to grow up. There were to be 10 years between the first and the last. First to be born was June in 1931, Pat in '33, Sheila in '41 and the last little Winson Greenite, Edward, in 1946. Sheila was born in this little back house during an air raid. Her dad worked at Tangyes at the time and was on fire watch. What a way to come off night shift, and so our little story of Sheila starts.

Being brought up a strict Catholic she would naturally go to a local Catholic school, this being St Patricks, fortunately as a day pupil unlike her mom. It would have been a long drag up the Green to go to school on the Dudley Rd, which is opposite Dudley Rd hospital. She learned something though from her mother in a roundabout way that love should pass on.

15

The area around where Sheila lived was a mixture of the usual terraced and back houses. Talbot St ran alongside Don St but was split with a little street called Harding St. All down now but from those days there is an host of memories for Sheila from that little spot. At this time Sheila's mom worked at the Bacchus Rd laundry and later at All Saints Hospital. (A better name than the 'Asylum') After working at Tangyes down Smethwick Sheila's dad went to work locally at Cheneys. In 1956 Sheila went there as well.

Her playground was the street and the back yards, she played with the Powells, Billy, David and Dennis. At other times it was to be the 'Rec' which lay between Talbot St and Musgrave Rd as it was on the doorstep, but it was still worth making that extra journey to Handsworth Park.

As Sheila went to a school that was a bus ride away from Talbot St her friends were pretty well spread out, Maureen Whelan came out of Clissold St, Brookfields, (and both remain good friends to this day) another was Annette Seal from the same area, Hingeston St. Susan Handlon came out of Victor Rd and Barbara Callan, whose father was a prison officer, lived in the prison houses lying under the walls of the prison in Lodge Rd. The only real local girlfriend was Anne Glennon, who lived down Lodge Rd by the Congregational Church. She was originally from Ireland and lived with her grandparents. There was one funny thing which always stuck in her memory and that was a friend that she played with. She lived just up from Talbot St, before the short cut up the steps to Bacchus Road, there were some more steps that led to another house. It was noticeable to Sheila at the time that the windows of her friend had the old fashioned coloured glazing of Stags and the M and B insignia on them, it doesn't seem like a pub, could it have been a very early off licence? who knows.

After leaving school Sheila went to work at Cheneys in Factory Rd as an assembler, they made fittings for high class suitcases, and they were a large employer in the area. Sheila's dad worked there, as well as Susan and her sister Margaret Handlon and Maureen Whelan. Later on she was to meet her husband to be, Dave Avery from out of Peel St. It was to be in Summerfield Park, a notable 'monkey run'. She was only 15 but it was to be match for many years to come, though courting was on and off, Sheila still went out with her mates. They were to get back together and married in 1960 at St Patrick's. They went to live in a flat in City Rd, no children were allowed, and unfortunately, or fortunately for them Sheila was expecting. They now had to look for somewhere else to live. They moved into a flat in St Peters Rd Lozells. After Ian was born, they moved out of Birmingham for pastures new, like many others at that time in the 60's, they as a family went to live in Brownhills, Staffordshire.

Sheila's Life though was Talbot St. It was part of her make up, and at that time this was her world. She remembers the area like all of us do theirs with clarity. As in the case of the patients getting out of the mental hospital and running up Lodge Rd being chased by the nurses.

Talbot St, although not very long had it's own pub, the Talbot , where Sheila's dad was a regular. There were a number of shops in this small street. One was Mrs Tibbits, whose son was a bookmaker, others were Flaherty's and Smith's. All these were the innumerable grocers! One shop in the street was different and that was a drapers which doubled up as a pawn shop. This was on the corner of Harding St. The little street between Talbot and Benson Rd did not have a shop.

Sheila Clemens on her wedding day.
(D Avery)

Coming down from Bacchus Rd to Don St, lay other little shops. There was a grocers, sweet shop and a butchers. Then came Don St. Not till I looked at a photo from the 50's did I realise that it was cobbled. The Don public house stood on the corner. It seemed to encroach on the houses in Lodge Rd and Don St, it was another notable pub in the darts and domino league. Houses only occupied this little street, it seems almost Dickensian. Today it seems romantic, but it must have played havoc in the snow and ice. Sheila told me of the shops that ran from Don St to

Musgrave Rd, an electric shop that accumulated batteries and a ladies' hairdressers. There was also a grocers which she said was run by a Welsh couple and a little drapers. Some of these shops, though forgotten now by their names, Sheila remembers so well.

We'll now leave Sheila and Talbot St to go up the Lodge Rd to Ted Rudge's patch and to visit Kent St North.

Don St. and Don Public House in the 1950s
(J Landon)

The Talbot as stands today in Talbot St.
(D Avery)

A MOVE TOWARDS THE 'FLAT'

Ted Rudge was one of the first to write to me when my first book came out. He addressed the letter to the 'Author' for which I felt very humbled. I got to know Ted and to his wife Maureen. I found out that she came from alien territory, as in Ladywood. (but people do marry out of the district) They now live in Solihull, rather more upmarket than the Green, but no less different than the majority of us that wanted more than a back yard and an outside lavatory. This is Ted's story as told by himself.

"Up to and including our generation, families did not move away from each other. Often couples from the same or nearby districts met, were married and went to live close to their old family home. I was a Winson Green lad and my wife Maureen came from Ladywood. Maureen's parents Stan and Doris Greensall were born, bred and after marrying were to set up home in Ladywood. Stan's parents though moved over the border to Devonshire St off the Lodge Rd. Doris's parents were married at St Chrysostems Church on the 20th of September 1902. Doris's father Thomas Wallis (Maureen's Grandfather, came out of Nelson St Ladywood and married Annie Eliza Worsey who lived then at 62 Preston Rd opposite Handsworth New Rd schools). The house still stands today. Thomas's occupation at the time was a boatman, that was our early connection with Winson Green, the links with Ladywood and the 'Green' were significant with generations of families coming together.

"Winson Green was our families' world; we lived both up the 'Green' and on the way down to the 'Flat'. My father John (or better known as Jack) worked at G.K.N. in Heath St. He was the eldest of 13 children. He was born in Oxford Square, Dugdale St. A one room down and two up terraced house.

(The house was featured in my book on page 12 of 'A Walk Up the Green', it was the one with the proverbial bath on the outside wall. I am informed this one was the actual bath which was used by the family! Ed.)

" How on earth did they manage? With great difficulty I should imagine, but manage they did. My mother (Margaret) did seem to be a little better off as she was the second born of three children, her parents were in ser-

19

vice (the butler and maid) before coming to live in a two up, three down, front house in Devonshire St.

"After my mom and dad got married they lived in Magdala St at first. John my elder brother was born there in 1938. Though me and my sister were to be born further along Lodge Rd in Kent St North. I was born nine months after the outbreak of war, and my sister Eileen two years later. Our little family was to be together only for a short time as our dad was killed on active service on the 6th February 1944 in Burma.

" Homes in the Kent St North were a mixture, on our side of the road we had Albert, Russell and Victoria terraces together with Malvern and Matlock Places, (posh sounding names, but posh they certainly were not) on the other side were court yards 1 to 8 and the best in the street was Clifton Terrace. A total of approximately a hundred homes. At best the houses could be described as adequate, although there was no hot water, no bathrooms, just shared lavatories, brew-houses and 'miskins'. The terraces were our playground, wonderful for hide and seek and the inevitable copping out when things got out of hand, like our house that had three steps coming from the front door, it was a meeting place for all of us kids. It was illuminated by the gas lamp in front of the house, many a bucket of water was passed under the door to break up the meeting! Our house was on the street, it was number 40, it fronted Russell Terrace, our coal cellar was always full of water, and before using the coal we had to dry it out. The house had a side and a front door, but the latter was always locked. Attached to our house were four more houses, like most others in the district, one room down and two up, off the passageways it led onto gardens at the rear, (if a patch of ground eight foot square could be classed as a garden!)

"Looking back, the adults who lived in the street always seemed kind and friendly. My first memories of the street are of being picked up out of bed, by somebody who wrapped me in a blanket. They ran with me up the street to what I now know was the air raid shelter. The shelter itself was under the garden of a big house on the corner of Lodge Rd, it must have been huge as it was used by the whole street.

"As children we tended to group or gang with others in our street. Kids from neighbouring streets were treated with caution. We played in the street from morning till night, up until the resounding shouts from our moms to come on in, and get ready for bed. At the Lodge Rd end of the street, were two long and very high walls either side of the horse-road.

This was to be our cricket square in the summer and a football pitch during the winter months. We were always on the look out for policemen when playing up the street, they were always around, though one day we were off our guard and got 'copped', we all finished up at Dudley Rd Police Station, our parents were sent for and we all received a good telling off for "playing football in the street!!" Much agro was always received when retrieving a ball which accidentally found it's way over the wall into the gardens of the big houses on either corner of the street.

"We lived in the middle of Kent St North, opposite our house was Kavanaghs coal yard, next door to them was Mrs Plume's shop, like many other small shops she sold everything, my memory of her was when the sweet rationing was on (that was most of my childhood) she declared to me "you can't have any as they'll make your nose bleed!" Another shop could be found at the Devonshire Avenue end of our street which was run by a Mrs Piper; I loved her boiled ham, I remember being sent one day by a neighbour for some 'Boil' beans and came out the shop with dried peas! Next door to Pipers, occupying the corner of Kent St and Devonshire Ave was an Ansell's house, styled as was many other pubs with glazed tiles, but these were white and stood out like a beacon, it was run by a Mr and Mrs Kemp, it was officially called the 'Princess Alexandra' but was affectionately known as the 'Alec' by the locals. Most nights the pub was packed out, football, dominos and darts teams competed from there. On the other corner was Jacksons fruit and veg shop, penny 'specs' could be bought from there but most times they were given for free if you asked nicely.

Small shops of all descriptions abounded in all working class areas, and made a living. They were the favourite places that I have remarked on, and that local people in an area would use as their main focal shopping centre, no more than the Rudge's should I add, and also to the people from this one particular area, but let's back to Ted's story.

"Shopping other than from local shops were mostly done on the 'Flat', where a gathering of 50 or more different shops could be found. Our mom shopped at the Co-Op on the corner of Heaton St, To this day I can still recall our number it was 249537 (ours is also still ingrained on my memory from those times 226637 Ed). Spencers the greengrocers with it's open front who also sold poultry, rabbits and wet fish from his shop next door. Boots the chemist, Woolworth's, Freeman Hardy and Willis the shoe shop, George Masons the grocers, Marsh and Baxters pork butchers and Sutcliffes who sold records, these were just some of many shops that I remember from that little bit of the flat part of Lodge Rd from Park Rd and Icknield St. Before leaving the 'Flat' I always wanted but did not always get, one of the best dripping cakes in the world, they could be bought from Cox's the bakers, with a toffee bottom, full of currants with a sugary top' the corner piece was the best, it makes my mouth water just thinking about it today. The shopping area was flat but the walk back to Kent St North was anything but!

"Lodge Rd at this point became a steep hill, starting off with the Post Office at the bottom and continuing up Lodge Rd passing Scribbans' bakery on the way. Many a Saturday was spent earning some pocket money by helping the roundsmen in delivering the bread, in those days the bread carts were pulled by horses. Up past Goode St the road still climbed laboriously on. Passing Abbey St and the Abbey Vaults pub, Paxton Rd and Harmer St, where stood in those days a small electrical shop, where we used to take our batteries to be accumulated. We were now coming to the top of the hill and passing by the British Oxygen, with it's huge stone Lion on top of the entrance to the factory, with one paw draped across a ball, which depicted the world, a reflection I suppose of past colonialism, I wonder what happened to that imposing stone Lion and where did it finish up?

Next we passed the one and only local phone box before starting off on our downward part of Lodge Rd. passing Tynegates the timber yard with the whining of the saws and the smell of fresh sawn timber. There was a cutting either side of the canal bridge at this point, leading to a towpath and the start of All Saints Hospital one side. Many a trip was made with an old pram or barrow down the other side of the road to fetch a quarter of a hundred weight of coal from the coal wharf. The Ford Motor research occupied the next building where once stood a glass works by the name of Welsh-Welsh. (Before that Shakespeare's Ed.) Thank God we were now going downhill, passing Norton St and in view of our street, we were now home and dry.

"Coming back up from our street is Norton St, it used to have an off licence which was handy for popping in for a packet of fags whilst waiting for the 96 bus, town the one way or the Green the other. Part the way down Norton St on the right hand side was Coveley Grove, it was built on the site of the old Norton St School. Most of the children from the area went to Benson Rd Schools but the books that were used still had the name Norton St School stamped on them, most confusing to the kids I'm sure.

The street crossed over the railway line, I had my first 'ciggy' on this bridge one night after Carol singing, and unfortunately carried on for the next 30 years. Before Bradfords bakery went up to West Bromwich opposite the Albion grounds it was situated in Norton St and the smell of fresh baked bread would waft all around, bread could be bought after 10 PM on a Sunday night. From the age of 10, starting at 5-30am on a Saturday morning I helped one of the bread delivery men on rounds all over Birmingham, finishing after 9-00 PM for the grand sum of seven shillings and sixpence.

"Back over the bridge you came to the one end of Devonshire St. On the corner was Davies, a drapers shop run by two ladies, lots of brown papers and ladies' things. Next door lived Mr and Mrs Greensall, later on in life they turned out to be my wife Maureen's grandparents, their garden over looked the railway line. A small shop that sold everything including a penny bottle of Vantos pop, (was it only in Birmingham where this strange tasting drink was sold? Ed) they even had a one armed bandit. In a house a few yards further down lived a man and his wife called Piggy (for the life of me I never found out why), he sold fresh mint and rhubarb from his back garden. Over the other side of the road was Sarah's owned by Mrs Jeavons the fish and chip shop. Sarah would let us kids eye the potatoes and hand chip them; we got paid a tanner and a bag of chips a night, any newspaper that wasn't torn up and put on the back of a lavatory door was welcomed at Sarah's, and for a big bundle we were rewarded with a bag of fried batter bits. Any customer who required change at the shop was given it from a purse that was kept up the leg of Sarah's knickers!

"Another two small shops a coal yard were passed then we came to Rowlands Electrical Accessories Ltd, (R.E.A.L.) a large building which employed a number of local people including my mother's sister Aunty Pem, she worked in the canteen and always waved when we went passed. Facing the R.E.A.L. was a builders yard owned by Bancroft's, then at the corner of Lees St was a Grocers by the name of Anscombe. Two more small shops could be found in Lees St and a pet shop (Morris's) on the corner of Lodge Rd facing the Congregational Church. Locally this church was known as the Institute, it held services, had its own Sunday school, a home to various youth organisations and once a year an Anniversary parade around the streets. Back at the other end of Lees St was an off licence on the corner of Devonshire St, houses ran the length of this street split by terraces on the one side which included my grandparents who lived at no. 86. Arriving at Lodge Rd there was a vegetable shop and a row of other little shops including a butcher, newsagent and yet another fish and chip shop. Crossing over and coming down Devonshire St various small shops stood hand in hand with terraced houses. As I've said the people were rough and ready but by and large very friendly, no more so than Mr Enoch Wassell, he was the local 'Tally Man' and was able to provide anything, he lived up one of the terraces on this side of the street, Mr Wassell was a very respected man who did a lot of good, always had a kind word to say to us youngsters when he was collecting his money.

"Before the days of legal bookmaking shops, illegal 'Bookies' plied their trade from where they could, none more than Tommy Harper, his blacked out shop on the corner of Devonshire St and Devonshire Ave was a magnet for anyone wishing to put a few bob on a horse or a dog. Many a time when taking a bet for a relative or a neighbour I got locked in when the police were expected, not only was he the local 'Bookie' he also owned a 52 seater Charabanc (coach) providing trips to the seaside from the local pubs in the area. (Similar to Sammy Small from out of Heath St, from A walk Up the Green, Ed.)

"Devonshire Avenue, contained some of the best houses in the area with gardens at the front on the railway side, a short distance in length from Musgrave Rd. With other large factory buildings on the each corner. Toogood's who made metal tubes and Samuel Groves' who did metal pressings, next to them was Linguards who produced children's clothes. Across the road was the 'Rec.' its actual title was Musgrave Road Recreation Ground, it even had its own 'Parky' self contained with his own hut and coal fire. The 'Rec.' was on two levels, the upper was grass and the bottom end was tarmac for games etc, but the bottom was grass, not for the kids to play on, but manicured for crown green bowling . If we had enough money the hire of the green plus the bowls and rubber could be ours, but more often than not we could only afford just to sit and watch other people play .

"Next to the 'Rec.' was 'The Gully' which ran from Musgrave Rd to Talbot St, it was very steep, it was a short cut but in the winter it was a different matter, after snowing it was to produce something like the Cresta Run' as a slide would be produced down the slope, no way could anybody walk up it without holding on to the railings, as kids we had great delight in watching adults attempt to walk up or down this path.

"Under the railway bridge in Musgrave Rd was our church, St

Chrysostoms. It was the church where our mom and dad got married in, and later on the three of us kids were to be christened. Later on I was to sing in the choir, I went to Sunday school and was a member of the youth club there. If it hadn't have been for the summer outings from the church we would never have left the 'Green'. It was the only holidays us kids had until we left school and started work.

"The careers officer at Handsworth New Rd Secondary Modern School asked me "whom" I would like to be employed by? My reply was the "Police Force"; say no more! My early working life was spent with the General Post Office as a (Wag) messenger boy delivering telegrams. I spent three years racing around the north of Birmingham on a B.S.A. Bantam motor bike provided by the Post Office, based in Key Hill Hockley, just up from the 'Flat'.

"Each of us three Rudge children eventually left Kent St North to get married; I had spent twenty years in that little house.

"When we had all gone our mom eventually left that house at the front of Russell Place and moved about twenty yards down the street into the next terrace for a bigger house with a front room and her own outside lavatory."

"That's progress"

Maureen left and Ted in the back garden of his mom's house in
Kent St. North
(T Rudge)

Telegram Messengers known as the 'Hockley Wags' 1958
Ted centred in the middle on his bike
(T Rudge)

"DON'T GET THOSE NEW CLOTHES DIRTY"

I wrote at length in my first book about my time at Handsworth New Rd school, but I feel that I need to bring this school back into this book as so many of the youngsters that came the area would remember their school days at this particular place.

Handsworth New Rd Secondary Modern School, what a mouthful, the school itself came and went in one century, it was opened in 1901 and closed during the 1980's. It even had an annexe which was at the rear of Bolton Rd Schools, at the top of Queens Head Rd, here was where we were taught metalwork, there were a few classrooms on the other side of the playground, but to get back to the main school it had learned it's lessons from the old board schools, in which the girls side was completely separate from the boys. On both sides the school was all on one level, apart from the science and woodworking block on the boys side, as the science room was over the woodworking area. As far as I remember there wasn't any connecting doors between the girls and boys school, so there was to be no hanky panky behind the bike shed!

In those days there were three types of schools in the city, the secondary moderns, technical and grammar schools. Though there were the secular schools as Catholic, C of E and other denominational schools. All had a place, if fortunate enough at the age of eleven the 11 plus could be attained, if not at the age thirteen other exams could be re-taken, and if successful go onto a technical school, many would do this and at Handsworth New Rd the pass rate was good, this showed the ability of the school in the advancement of particular pupils. This piece though is of myself and perhaps of many others that would pass through those school gates.

The long hot summer had come to an end, it was coming into autumn, down the Black Patch Park. The leaves on the trees were turning gold and there was nip in the air, though not like the chill that I had in the pit of my stomach, it was time to go to the big school, and for days I had been dreading this one particular morning.

The bed held me like a magnet, I didn't want to get up, a voice boomed up the stairs "Com'on are you gettin' up, you'll be late for school?". I didn't want to go, shall I tell her that I don't feel very well? I realised at that young age that it would be a waste of time. Slowly I dragged myself out of bed and made my way down stairs into the parlour, the lino was cold to my feet but not as cold as our mom. "It's five and twenty past eight, and you ain't got your clothes on yet" On the kitchen table was a box of cereals and a bottle of 'Sterra' I never drank tea only a cup of milk, I poured some milk into a cup and the rest over the cornflakes, our mom was busy up the sink but still kept on about getting myself dressed, in between mouthfuls of cornflakes I started getting ready, a clean white shirt, new trousers and a sports jacket, the shoes were gleaming, it wasn't until a year or so later that we had to wear the regulation uniform. Eventually I was ready and our mom looked me up and down and in a softer accent said that I should do, but her parting shot as I was walking out of the door was "Don't you dare get them clothes dirty". She hadn't got to tell me, I didn't fancy having a good hiding when I came home from school. Out of the back door and down the entry I went, at the bottom Jeff Hughes was waiting for me, Ronnie Beaman had already gone as he had to go and get the number11 bus to City Rd as he had passed for George Dixon's Grammar school, we now were two, and a couple of years later I would be on my own going to school as Jeff passed his exams for Handsworth Technical School. We made our way up Foundry Rd past our old junior and infants school with all of the kids milling about the entrance, time was running out by now and hurrying round the corner into Handsworth New Rd joined the throng which were making their way to our new school, they seemed to come from everywhere, from up the Green, out of Lodge Rd, from Markby, Willis and Preston Roads and down the hill from Ninevah Rd, they were all starting a new term. The gates came into view and all these kids were funnelling through one set of double gates, we passed through with plenty of pushing and shoving from the older ones, we kept ourselves to ourselves, the big lads looked huge and their reputations preceded them, the bell went and we all lined up to go inside, the smell of a new school with the polish that will stick with me for ever, and so a new chapter in mine and countless other youngsters from the Green was to start. I shan't go into any more detail as I've already written about it once, but I bet it invokes the reader in remembering this school or others similar.

I pass the building now quite often, it's still there, I think it is now a day centre of sorts, but you know I can still here that bell ringing, the teachers shouting at kids to stop running in the corridor, the fear of the cane, and actually having it, the 'swoosh' as it came down and the numbness when it was over, teachers who tried at times to install some sort of education into us. It was long time ago I know but I will never forget that first day. It will always stick with me.

Just a post-script to this chapter, a short time before I finished this book, an aunt of my wife, Gladys James, died in hospital in Tamworth. In talking to her remaining cousin from Brighton, he mentioned that he had her school leaving certificate from 1930, the remarkable thing was a letter (hand written, of course) from her last teacher, it was a reference to any future employer, the signature at the bottom made me smile and wince at the same time, it was none other than George Liddle, our old head at Handsworth New Rd, he was a teacher at Leigh Rd Council School in Small Heath. It was the date that intrigued me. The following year he was to play for Birmingham City F.C. at Wembley against West Bromwich Albion, and then back to a teacher, or was he a part timer for the Blues?

Looking down towards Bishop Latimers.
The school is on the left hand side, past the houses.
(A Dolman)

WHAT A FAMILY !

A lot of us Brummies have sat and listened to this man. His repertoire and renderings of on our own city. He's done the rounds and can proudly wear the tee-hirt. His name is Laurie Hornsby.

The first time I met him was in the Bull Ring. Carl Chinn was doing a book signing, and on a bit of a stage Laurie was doing his bit on the guitar, and promoting his latest recordings. I wanted to speak to him as my two aunts from out of Wellington St knew his mothers side of the family . They worked at Settern and Derwards in Benson Rd. They knew Laurie as a young lad and over the years would see him grow older, they asked me to pass on their regards if ever I should meet him. I did. This was to be an eventful meeting as far as I was concerned. I didn't realise that I should meet not only this charming guy but also his dad, Bill. His smile never left his face the whole time I was with him, no wonder his lad's the same and what a story they both told me.

Although Laurie doesn't hail from the Green where his mom's parents lived, I can't help but bring a little bit of Handsworth into the picture. Let's start with his dad Bill.

Bill's dad was born in Whitmore St at the bottom end of Park Rd. His father was a clockmaker and originated from Rugby. They moved away from Birmingham to Leamington Spa and Rugby to follow his trade for a time, and then later moved back to live in Camden St. Laurie remembers sitting on his grandad's lap as a child and being told how things were much harder then, even to the fact of working for the local newsagent taking papers. The newsagent felt sorry for this little lad as he hadn't any warm clothes and the newsagent put brown paper between his 'Ganzie' and his coat to keep out the cold in the winter, even as far as stuffing cardboard in his shoes! Anyway Bill's dad moved out of Winson Green after he got married and went live at no 45 Mary Rd Handsworth where Bill and his sister Millicent were born. He went to Bolton Rd and Handsworth New Rd Schools and left at the grand age of 14.

His first job was a plumbers mate at Derby's the builders in Tew Park Rd, and he learned to grow up quickly. The plumber who he mated was a nasty piece of work, and had a succession of mates who left him. Even after the first week Bill was adamant that he wasn't going to go back to work with this plumber. His dad played lights out but Bill stuck his ground. Anyway the next morning came a knock on the door and it was the plumber. In an apologetic tone "Com'on Bill, I'm losing 1/6 an hour". Like a fool Bill went back. But things didn't change. At that time they were putting up cast iron guttering in Mere Green, and because Bill was young and keen , he had tightened up the brackets a bit too hard and cracked the guttering. The air turned blue and the plumber threatened to throw him off the scaffolding. Bill felt the ladder underneath him move and this little old lady of perhaps 70, popped her head over the scaffold boards. "Young man" in an evidently haughty voice, "If I hear you speak to that boy again in that manner, it will be me that will be throwing you off the scaffold".

They finished the job and in a cursory tone told Bill to take the tools home with him that night as they were going to start another job on the Saturday morning at Wylde Green, and bring them back on the job. Bill was only little lad and to carry this huge bag of plumbers tools on three buses from Sutton all the way back over to Handsworth was the last straw. He made his way to the Builders yard, instead of going home first, he went up the stairs to the gaffer's office and demanded his cards and his money. The gaffer went barmy but Bill stuck his ground, Bill was told that this partic- ular plumber had had a roasting in the week for his attitude, and was warned that he wouldn't have another mate if Bill left. But it didn't make any difference, Bill was going, he waited till he had his money and his cards and off he went. Bill though had the last laugh though, because now the plumbers tools were at the yard, and the plumber who lived in Great Barr would go on the job on the Saturday morning at Wylde Green, and find there would be no Bill and certainly no tools, as this huge bag was in Tew Park Rd Handsworth. Everything comes to those that wait!

Bills next job was at Bulpitts as a tinsmith till he went into the navy. During the war he courted a girl by the name of Dolly Davis, she and her parents lived in Douglas Rd Handsworth till they got bombed out, and went live in Brunswick Gardens in Brunswick Rd. They were married on the fifth of July 1946, at St James' Church in Crockets Rd. They had their do at Watville Rd Schools, and went to live with his in-laws. They put their names down on the forces register, even now Bill still remembers his registration number it was 32760, and to this day he's still had no reply!

At this time Bill and his father in law weren't getting on to well, and in

1950 with a bit of help from money left by his own dad, he put a deposit on a house in Malvern Rd.

Time at Brunswick Gardens with his in-laws wasn't always without it's laughs. At that time milk was always delivered by a horse and cart, and Laurie remembers so well that one particular horse would wait till he came up Brunswick Rd and would relieve itself. It would always drop its load outside a Mrs Matthews' house, she would run outside and shout to the poor horse . "Find yourself a new spot" in an indignant tone, but the horse at the same time on the day after would do it all over again.

After working at the Coventry Radiator for a time till being made redundant, Bill felt that he didn't want to work in a factory again, and after moving to Malvern Rd he went with his father in law cleaning windows. They cleaned windows around the Soho Rd. Banks, shops, houses and even the Regal Cinema. Things though weren't going that well between the two men, and Bill sacked his father in law. While Bill was cleaning the windows, the old chap was always in the coffee house in Grove Lane, supping tea and making out his bets!

In between all this Laurie was born on the 1st May 1948 in Dudley Rd Hospital. He was to start his life in Brunswick Gardens and a couple of years later move to Malvern Rd. He attended Watville Rd School, and was a prominent footballer as shown in the football team photo. He was a keen footballer and naturally played for the school, the biggest opponents were Foundry Rd, and they played on the Black Patch, and guess where Watville Rd schools pitch was, the same, so who ever was at home, or away, they always knew where to go, if I remember rightly there was more dirt than grass, it was to be a fitting name.

Laurie though went on to pass his 11 plus and went to George Dixons in City Rd. At sport the round ball stopped and was to be replaced by an oval one, and to this day Laurie hates the game of rugby. Also his time at George Dixons he loathed from day one.

The Allen's Rd connection was naturally through Bill's wife. It was a massive family. The front door to the house was used more than New St Station. There were three brothers and eight sisters, these were the immediate children of the Emery's. Lauries mom, Doris was the daughter of Mabel, one of the eight.

The sisters were Minnie, Hilda, Winnie, Ethel, Marjorie, Lillie, Mabel and Ethel. The brothers were Len, Horace and Alan, unique in the fact that they married three sisters from out Camden St by name of Hodgkiss.

Bill Hornsby and others told me tales of this family. There was one sister by the name of Winnie she did more moving around the area than a Pickfords van and for a time lived in our street, Eva Rd. Hilda, another sister used to accompany backward children to school, she talked with an affected posh accent till she let it slip, like the one time she was with these kids and bumped into Bill as he was on his window cleaning round " Now come on now, I don't want to be here all day, or I'll clip your *bleedin'* ears". Laurie was one of 48 grand children! Minnie's son Derek, who was Laurie's cousin, was never allowed to go to Grove Lane baths during the summer. He would be sitting on the step crying, when everybody else was going swimming, Aunt Minnie's words were "It's no good you cryin', you can't go to the baths till you can learn to swim"! Her husband was named Alfred but was better known as 'Olf'. Now he was only a small bloke and with all the family one Saturday night in the Barrel Pub on the Main Rd, a fight broke out in the passage in Louise Rd, 'Olf' had always been bragging how hard he was and said "I'll go and sort 'em out", he'd only got his shirt on and less than half a minute later came flying back into the bar with it hanging off his back. The room was in silence. Not saying a word, he walked up to the bar and broke down crying. As I said he was only a little chap so I suppose they took a pity on him!

Then there's Laurie in his big hearted way, which I can say to this day, thought he would help his uncle out on his honeymoon arrangements. Tony was his mother's brother, only a few years older than Laurie, and was asked to be his best man. Tony had told Laurie that he was going to Jersey and wanted to stop at the Merton Hotel. This was a big swanky hotel that was the bees knees, It was the honeymoon hotel of the island and had the grand ballroom with the cocktails and evening dress. It was going to cost upwards of £200 and it was going to skin him, Laurie in his infinite wisdom, said "I've got a mate that works for Doug Ellis the travel agent in Cannon St down the town, I'll see what I can do for you". Well Laurie went along to see his mate and told him, after a short while he came back to Laurie and told him that he had got them fixed up for a fiver a night. Laurie went back to Tony and told him the good news, feeling very proud of himself. Tony told Laurie to get it fixed up, well this was going to be a big surprise to his wife to be as she didn't know anything about it.

Well the day of the wedding came and Tony married Jill Short from out of Willis Rd. The reception was held at the church hall in Austin Rd off Holyhead Rd, Tony though had to smuggle into the reception all of Jill's dresses that she would need for the Merton, there was to be the cocktail dresses, matching shoes and handbags and so on, so that she wouldn't suspect, as they were going to spend their honeymoon night at the Midland Hotel down the town.

The wedding went off well and they duly stopped the night at the Midland in the town and the next day they had a taxi to the old airport at Elmdon and took off for Jersey, so far so good. After landing at Jersey they were met by a rep from Ellis Travel and was taken by taxi to St Heliers and this is where it went all pear shaped. It was right they were going to the Merton, but this wasn't *the* Merton, but Mrs Merton's Guest House, which was a 50 bob a night affair and have to be in at 10 pm. It was to be a disaster, they couldn't get any thing to eat and had to resolve to eating a bag of fish and chips on the corner of the street. After all the intrigue of smuggling Jill's clothes into the taxi after the wedding reception Tony's dreams must have gone from bad to worse. This wasn't the end of the story though. Whilst stopping at the Midland on their wedding night, the following morning as they waited for the the taxi to take them to the airport, Tony was in the lounge of the hotel and started to watch some sport that was on the TV, after a few minutes a chap in a white jacket came in and in a polite voice informed Tony that he was going to take the TV away, well it was as you can imagine a rather large TV that a hotel like the size of the Midland would have had. The man in the white coat was struggling with it and Tony said would he like an hand with it, the man was very grateful, and so they made their way through the foyer into New St and put it into this chap's car, and off he went. Tony thought no more about it. After going back into the lounge the manager came in and with a look of surprise asked Tony where the TV was and Tony duly told of a man in a white coat coming in, unplugging the set and taking it outside into his car, the man, naturally was a blatant thief, it was if it this was an omen for the Honeymoon.

This little story of the Hornsby's as I've said is not wholly of Winson Green, but a make up of our neighbours from Handsworth, and how much all of our friends and relatives came from our small area.

'What a Family?
Group photo in Allens Road
(L Hornsby)

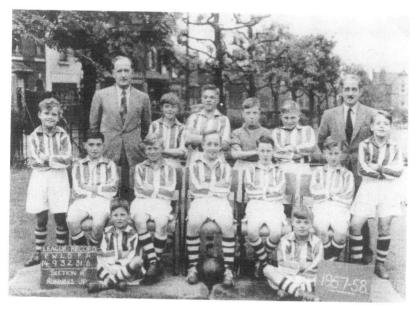

Watville Road School Junior Football Team
(Laurie bottom right)
(L Hornsby)

A Family Wedding at 'New Inns', Holyhead Road, Handsworth.
(L Hornsby)

WAS IT A SHOP OR A FRONT ROOM ?

Wherever there was a street there would be the inevitable shop, be it on a corner or in the middle of a row of terraced houses. Why? There were always the shops and markets on the main roads and town centres, why though in the middle of built up districts? I suppose that as there were always the entrepreneurial amongst those that settled into an area, or someone handed down their little business in the family, it has always intrigued me, it wasn't as if there was no competition, there was, numerous shops in the same street would have sold the same tin of beans as a loaf or a pound of sugar. Was it a shop as I've said, or a front room?

Throughout my growing up and early working life I was to see many hundreds of these same establishments, I was born in a typical working class area as we all know. In our street there were four shops, there was one before on the corner of Eva Rd and Foundry Rd, but I don't remember it being open, only that a family named the Beards lived there, they didn't alter the front windows and it always looked like a shop, but I'll come back in some small way to my street later on.

After leaving school I became a member of the retailing trade, what a grand sounding name for a 'Bread Lad'. The round which I was on was a lot more 'posh' than the district that I had been brought up in. It was Quinton. The shops were more organised, there was, and still is the main shopping centre at the bottom end of the Hagley Rd West, up at the top of Ridgeacre Rd, and some at the end of Worlds End Lane, there were others though at the top end of Quinton by Four Dwellings schools. These were shops that had been thought about when the districts were formed, they were all very orderly, not like the variety of shops that I had known. Naturally there was the Green , the 'Flat' and the 'Main Rd', and not to mention the Dudley Rd. Amongst all of these were the locals, they provided what the larger shops could not do, that was to give 'Tick', I'm not saying that all the folks that frequented these little establishments didn't pay as they bought , but they were okay for a good many that hadn't the coppers till pay day. The shopkeeper may have put a few coppers on the weekly bill, that was to be expected, some though would run a bill up with one shop, and then another, would pay off Jack and run up another

37

bill with Jill. But getting back to the theme, how did they exist. Okay they did charge a copper or more, they couldn't buy in bulk like their larger cousins, their profit margins were smaller, but what they did was to provide a service and they did it all right, I'll use an imaginary shop that would have been down any street and remember that they really did exist.

The over heads were nil, this after all was an house, and the front parlour was created into a shop. Outside surrounding the window enamelled signs would be telling all of the virtues of drinking Typhoo Tea in their own particular colours, as well as Mason and Tizer pops, and if sold tobacco, 'Players Please' and 'Digger Flake'. Inside the shop we were welcomed with bare boards, which were mopped daily and swept frequently. A large wooden counter ran just behind the door and turned at right angles towards the living quarters. It was imposing, the counter took up most of the shop, behind the counter was a vast amount of shelves, and what could be put on them was nobody's business. Imagine a large store with vast amounts of space to show and sell their goods, well the little street shops did their best with a fraction of the room for what there was, either side of this little shop was a normal house with perhaps a three-piece suite (if lucky), scatter rugs and in some cases a piano. But the owner of this shop would do with the back parlour and a small kitchen for their private use, the shop would come first, perhaps over the years the shop might make enough money and the shopkeeper hopefully retired without having thoughts of opening all hours.

Like I said I had served many such humble shops whilst on my travels, and all with the same surroundings as you entered the shop, the brass bell mounted on a coiled spring, when the door was opened a ringing would vibrate around this little emporium, out would come the owner, either she in a wrap round pinafore, or he in a brown cowgown, more often than not it was the former. Looking around the shop there was everything. If you couldn't see it no doubt it could be found by the owner, no freezers, all you wanted was either in a tin or dried, unlike their larger cousins, small shops were prepared to sell half a pound of rice for a pudding, a pound of sugar, even the little shop at the bottom of our entry, Kershaws, would sell half a loaf, cut within millimetres, practice made perfect. Tins and jars of sweets stood out like beacons on the shelf behind the counter next door to Victory V lozenges, also for upset stomachs was a bottle of Indian Brandy, but taking your own cup for sixpence a dose was the norm. Odd items for coughs and colds were close by, Aspirin, Beecham's Powders and other pills and potions that were in the main harmless.

Shelves would start from the floor and reach to the ceiling, bottles of pop and crates of milk were the closest to the floor, as well as bottles of bleach, disinfectants and ammonia, for wash days Rickets Blue bags, Robin Starch and big blocks of white or green soap, for personal hygiene were the carbolic or Lifebuoy soaps, and for the men razor blades and sticks of shaving soap. After shave and deodorants were a thing of the future, though you could go into the more high class chemist and get Eau-de Cologne, but I can't remember any men down our street going to this bother, just a good wash up the sink and a shave, but to get back to the shop, crisps would come in tins, always Smith's, greased proof packets with a little bag of salt inside. To survive shops would have to carry all sorts of stock for their customers, coal fires were the norm and this little shop provided help to get the fire started, on the floor stood little bundles of firewood tied up with wire, boxes of firelighters to get them started, only you had to provide your own newspaper to draw the fire, (if set alight, whoosh, as the paper was drawn up the flu and you would hope that it wouldn't set the chimney alight). Even to buying a mousetrap or to get a roll of sticky fly paper which always hung from the light shade.

Food was the main seller in the shop and tins of food were displayed alongside jars of pickles, bottles of sauces and jars of jam, salt could be bought in boxes but was also sold as a block the size of a loaf of bread, cheese was kept under a cotton gauze frame, as was the butter. As I've said they were the little cousins to the larger stores and needed to keep a vast amount of stock, it would encroach into their living quarters but that was a small price to pay. They were prepared to open up at all hours, and like this shop, all around hundreds of others were doing the same.

Some were a little larger and would have a double frontage, this would allow them to sell other things such as greengrocery, some shops though, were, as we would now say, for the niche market, only selling sweets, toffee apples and ice cream etc. These shops were up the smaller streets, on the busier roads were the newsagents, ironmongers and the like.

I come back to my street as I know these shops, Kershaws, Lotties', Groves's and at the top Eccles. These were no different or anything special as in any other street, as I found out in the years to come when I worked for Masons the pop people, A different area, another district all with their own little convenience 'store', they were there in all their glory, all providing a remarkable service and all selling from the the 'front room'.

Shops down Park Road towards the 'Flat'
(J Landon)

A TALE OF A TRAVELLER

On the next page I have drawn, I hope, a little word sketch of possibly a forefather of ours, his name is made up, but the roads and streets are not, as was the factory that he worked in, the man is fictitious, but his life as others were to find wasn't, it was possibly how a good many of us began in this great city of ours, some aspiring to greater things, others just happy to know that they were comfortable. At the end of the day we were all to be in some small way just like this traveller. His name, John Long.

FROM THE TOWN TO THE COUNTRYSIDE

In my last book I wrote a short piece on what it would have been like for someone who had made his way up Springhill passing the building of the new workhouse, to cross the top of Winson Green Road knowing that the new Borough Gaol was just down the road, and to continue his walk down to Smethwick. Well this time we are going from another direction to Birmingham Heath. Let's go a bit further in history than the 1850s, this time to the middle of the 18th century. We'll call our traveller John Long, our picture of him living on the outskirts of the town and making his way to his new employers on the edge of Birmingham and Handsworth Heath. It was Boulton's new works.

At about this time there were in excess of 23,000 people living in or around 3,500 properties so we can see for the paramount reasons that the town would have to grow, and not just for people but for business.

John Long was 26 years of age, and his wife a year younger, their parents had come from the countryside to earn a better living in this town. John's father was a blacksmith by trade and there were no shortages of jobs. Birmingham was growing and would need all the smithies that they could get. John Long though didn't want to follow in his fathers footsteps, as other trades were building up in the town. As a boy he was indentured into a brass firm, he was to learn the skills of buckle making, it was a little factory in Snow Hill. Even though steel was being produced from two new factories in the town, one close by in White Hall (Steel House Lane today) he chose to stop at the former. Steel was a new thing and buckles were made of it. Not so pliable as brass but when finished it would come up brighter and it kept its shine longer.

Boulton had a factory in Snow Hill but needed more room to expand, what better than unproductive land out on the heath, and so our little bit of a story of John Long enfolds.

After Boulton's Manufactory had been opened, word travelled fast as experienced brass workers would be needed. John made the journey to this new factory and got a job. His wage would be the large sum of eight shillings a week, in the town rates were more competitive with children doing the work of grown men for less money, it was also to be a lot different with not having to work in crowded conditions.

He needed this money as he had a wife and four children to provide for, this was the incentive to make his move from the town. He and his wife Florence had four children, John, Mary, Emily and James the youngest, there would have been six but one died at childbirth and the other one at a few months. They were lucky in holding on to four as housing and poor sanitation didn't help in rearing a family, they lived in Hall St off Great Hampton St. It was a typical cottage, not the sort with roses round the door, but cramped and over occupied, a pump provided water to a number of houses and a night closet was emptied by the parish. Foremost in his mind was the thought that if he kept his job at his new workplace he might get one of the workman's cottages that were being built around the factory, and therefore to save the long walk to work every morning and back home at night. He was a man with little education but with a great amount of endeavour, and so our journey follows.

The time as five thirty a.m., it was early summer and the light streaming through the window helped him to get up, he arose from their bed without trying to wake up Florence. She had been up in the night with James, he was only 18 months old and had been crying with a stomach ache, James had settled down and Florence was now fast asleep, in the other bedroom the other remaining children were still sound asleep. John made his way down the creaking stairs trying not to wake up the house, to the single parlour room where he got dressed. He cut himself a piece of bread and chewed it whilst he got himself dressed, he put on his breeches and boots, he tucked his shirt and buckled up his belt, it was a warm morning and he didn't need to put his only coat on, he wore a wide brimmed hat that was well worn and sweat marked. He cut another couple of slices of bread and a lump of cheese, the cheese was always kept under some muslin cloth on a cold slab, this was for his lunch, he wrapped these mere morsels up in a clean piece of cloth and knotted it, it was now time to go to work.

He opened the door as quietly as he could without waking the whole household, slowly closing it behind him, he made his way from his house to the corner of Gt Hampton St, a coach caught his eye as it made it's way into the town, it was the Holyhead to London coach, carrying mail, parcels and a few paying passengers, it was the reign of George the Third, it was to be another 80 years till Victoria came to the throne and the post was to be sent by rail. Other people were up and about now and making their way to work, it was a Monday morning and many a bleary eye passed him by, even though the area was slowly being built up, tracts of land were still being cultivated, either as gardens or earlier types of allotments.

Crossing Hockley St houses were beginning to peter out and countryside was becoming more prevalent, from the high ground he could see across the heath, birds singing high in the sky, the road in front began to slope down towards the Hockley Brook, but he didn't go along this way, he turned off to the left from Gt Hampton St down Tookey's Hill past the farm from which it took it's name. After crossing Icknield St, to his left lay Hockley Pool, still and mysterious in the morning light, the only thing moving were ducks and waterfowl, on the other side of the road were some cottages, smoke was gently drifting up in the morning air from the nearest one, John thought to himself if only he could live down there. The lane flattened out and he could see the split of the road ahead, on his left was the Blue Coat School surrounded by it's own gardens, the hill now began to rise and would take the right-hand one, this way was to the Ninevah, the other was to a small hamlet on Birmingham Heath called Winson Green. The journey along this lane took him past, what he thought was an abbey ruin, were he to know the real truth he would be well surprised. Now he met up with fellow workers making their way to the factory, they came mostly from Aston Manor and the surrounding districts, though others that came from the other way were from Staffordshire with their knowledge of the iron trade. They all enjoyed their work at this new factory, they worked for a gentleman with better thoughts for his employees and a better environment, not some local sweat shop back in the town. Together they walked past the Lodge house and the entrance to the estate, past the Soho Pool, which was more like a lake, and looking up at the masters house on the hill. The ground continued to climb till they came to a cross-roads, turning right made their may down the lane to the entrance of Boulton's Manufactory, and proceeded to go to their respective workplaces. It was a long way to come but John was glad of the chance to better himself.

His day completed, it was now seven o'clock and he was to make the return journey back home. Walking past the canal wharf he watched the boatmen loading goods which had been made where he came from, knowing in his own little gleaning of knowledge that these were to go all over the country, nay, the world. Back down the flat part of the lane, past the pool with the falling sun glinting across the water, up the hill past the farm, watching the herdsman driving the cattle in, into Gt Hampton St for the last leg of his journey, and finally back home to Florence and his children.

Perhaps there was a John Long, I don't know, but there must have been many like him who wanted something more for their families, to strive, to endeavour, to want and most of all to better themselves. The likes of our fictitious John Long's really did exist. They and thousands more after him would be prepared to make our town into a city.

Looking down Key Hill in the 1950s.
(J Landon)

Constitution Hill to the left and Hampton St
on the right from the bottom of Snow Hill
(J Landon)

THE GOD OF WINE COMES TO THE GREEN

Bacchanalia wasn't in the fore front when this road was first thought of. Strange the way that the town fathers were to name their streets. Local dignitaries, famous generals, notable townsfolk were always the prior credential. Odd names cropped up, either a geographical location or one that suited an area. Why Bacchus? presumably to counter the name of Ninevah just across the border at Handsworth Heath which was then in Staffordshire, the former Roman and Grecian the latter Arabian. No matter the name had been given, it was to come off the Lodge Rd and make it's way towards Handsworth, it was to be called a lane but finished up a road.

There had been smallholdings in the area for possibly hundreds of years dotted about in a rural community. Not till the district began to develop with the building of the asylum and prison was there to be serious housing development, with housing there was a need for cleanliness and I suppose this is where to the public washing baths came into being, but why this particular area, apart from the baths in Grove Lane Handsworth I can't think of any as local. During the latter part of the 19th century this like all of the rest of the Green it was to be developed, though not so crowded and littered with back to backs as was prevalent up the top end of the Green and down into Ladywood and Hockley, but there were the usual back houses, or as people would remark villas and places, according to whether they came from one of the street facing houses, or up an entry. Mostly the houses from the prison down were more in the way of villa type properties either in the case of Willis, Markby and Preston Roads with tiny front gardens and large ones at the back. This followed the case down Bacchus Rd to the border with Handsworth. We'll start with the make up of the road with it's shops, businesses and pubs. The numbers of the houses and the like ran from one to 101 at the bottom of Bacchus Rd and came back up on the other side from 102 to 227, it must have been a nightmare for any delivery man new to the area hoping to find an appropriate number on the opposite side of the road!

From the corner of Lodge Rd going down Bacchus Rd on the right hand side was Beaumont Terrace backing onto Binnell's fruitier and greengrocers next door was William Brannan who kept the local hairdressers, the public washing baths came next.

After an act of Parliament in 1846 local councils across the country were made to provide swimming and washing baths for the public, even though before then there were private establishments in the town for washing, but true to the Victorian ethos for cleanliness, washing baths were to be built for the populous, some incorporated swimming with washing, Bacchus Rd though was one that was built purely for washing, it was very well used over the many years of it being opened, fired from huge coke boilers at the rear of the premises, a promise of a well scrubbed bath with bags of hot water, to the locals from the area it was better than the tin bath in front of the fire, though in the winter you had to make sure that you were well wrapped up before coming out of from this establish-ment, all hot and well scrubbed, though it was better to take your own towels with you, as the towels, though clean and pressed were very rough, as a lad for one and sixpence it was my Friday night trip, so much for my memories. Let's continue down Bacchus road.

Next door to the baths was the local 'Rock' shop ran by Miss Harthill, other little businesses ran down to Benson Rd, Mrs Thomas who kept a grocers, then came Albert Yeomans the butchers and Harold Barnes the bread shop, then came Caines the florist and Smiths who ran his own chemists, Mr and Mrs Fox who kept the cafe, this was the last of the shops till after Allens Rd, after the cafe came the City Disinfecting Station, this in itself was another matter for cleanliness, upon the opening of the Borough Hospital in 1859 for the treatment of fever patients, such as Smallpox etc. at the old Fever Hospital at the top of Lodge Rd, it was decided that a treatment station be set up for the cleaning of clothes and bed linen from infected housing, this possibly carried on, but in a reduced situation as over the years when housing and living conditions improved.

Close by on the corner of Benson Rd was the City Laundry. Was there a correlation between the two?

The road started to slope down now after crossing the railway, Allens Road came next, it was split by Bacchus Rd, it finished up as a cul-de-sac overlooking the railway, it was known as little Allens Rd to the locals on the left hand side, the other way ran into Benson Rd. In between Allens Rd and Leonard St, was Chegwyn Products who supplied coachbuilders with their products, and a small grocers ran by Mrs Lewis, after Leonard St apart from a few houses down to the railway bridge was Bickleys house decorators, and the last was May Raxter who kept the off-licence, to the reader that didn't know the area would think that this road didn't have any houses, only shops etc. well in between was well over 100 private dwellings, and that was only on the one side of 'Bacchus'.

Coming up from the Railway bridge which spanned Bacchus and Park Rd the numbers of the properties ran the other way round which I have said, first of the business' was Buckley's the upholsterers, Emily Lowe who kept the greengrocers, Yvonne the ladies hairdressers, Bill Bailey the tobacconist and Louisa Savory for a nice bunch of flowers to be had from her shop. Then came The Grapes Public House, I would have been about 16 when I first went in there, I have always looked older than my real age as I've said, and we, Roy Richards, Bob Dolman and Jeff Hughes would go in there, if I remember we drank Sam Browns and played darts, we kept our heads down, there wasn't any trouble, the smell of the barman's apron was enough for us. It was a long time ago, but I'm a sucker for memories. Further up the road was the British Legion Club, it was later to move down the road to the opposite side, when the new building was built. Just before Allens Rd was a drapers, well known to many by the name of Mrs Moore. Crossing over Allens Rd Mr and Mrs Such kept a grocers and next to them was the nursery, it was known as the City Nursery School, it was a prefabricated building and many from the area knew it well, memories of the children who went there must be numerous, the view from the rear of the building was over the railway lines from the old G.W.R. the view was, as we would say today, panoramic, being so high up it looked over Handsworth all the way down to Smethwick and the Gasometers! On the corner of Willes Rd and Bacchus Rd was Harold Roath the newsagents, on the other side of the road was Trumans the boot and shoe repairers, followed by another shop belonging to the fruitiers, Binnell's, which kept one across the road by the baths, Markby Rd came and on the opposite corner was Bunnies the ladies hairdressers followed by George Parrott another small grocer, following on came Preston Rd and on the opposite corner was the Post Office. Between Preston and Kirkby, which was a cul-de-sac, a host of shops stood. There was another confectioner, Whitehouses, a fish and chip shop owned by Rose Taylor. Logue Jnr. a furniture dealer, Bill Richards the butcher, Franklin's kept another coffee house, another little grocer by the name of Dot Harwood, not only shops but a business with a grand sounding name of Albert Preece Jnr. Electrical Engineers. We now come towards the end of Bacchus Rd, but in between Kirkby and Lodge Rd, was the proverbial Co-Op with it's Grocers and dry cleaners occupying two shops, sandwiched between Powells the paper shop and the Lodge Garage, and a small company called E Gould's who worked in metal. The businesses we've now been to,

The Nursery, Bacchus Road - Home from home for many a toddler
(B Boscott)

Coronation St Party (Where? possibly down the Bacchus Road area)
(R Clarke)

we now need to find out some more from those who lived in the area Barbara Boscott grew up in this road, she wasn't always a Boscott, she was an Allen, she lived at 38 Bacchus Rd, with her dad Edward and her mother Ivy, her mom at the time of writing this book is 80 and like a lot of women as I've said worked at Settern and Derwards, but lets get back to Barbara, as in all working class districts family were all around, Charles and Norma Harvey lived at no 33, another aunt and uncle and cousin Kenneth lived at 39. They lived in the block of houses opposite the nursery, one of the neighbours lived in a double fronted house, the lady in question ran an hairdressers from there, her name was Hall and Barbara would play with her daughter Jean whilst her mom had her hair done, she remembers with clarity of the shops, and most of all the names that went with them, Jack Westwood kept the Post Office in Bacchus Rd, and in 1957, a thing though not heard of then, an overdraft, with the book still around to prove it, He allowed Barbara to draw out more than she had got in, he probably got a rollicking for not noticing how much she had remaining in her savings account! Albert Yeomans the butchers who had a farm at Hampton Loade and produced his own meat there, and sold it in his shop, and the memory of the garage on the corner of Lodge Rd, and the owner, Roy, who accidentally electrocuted himself. The area was full of memories not only of this girl but for many others, of their thoughts of days gone by with the likes of Bert Draper the licencee of the Talbot and his wife who made wonderful faggots, of Tonks' the coal merchants in Harding St, The Jolly Bacchus better known as the Grapes, these are not to be forgotten as of Barbara's uncle Sam Coley who played the piano at the Talbot pub for many years. The stories abound of the characters and the growing up around there, with the sound of a name or a shop the mind will bring back vivid memories, we'll meet Barbara again at school at Benson Rd but we now go to another girl that came from this part of the Green and was to live in Perrot St.

Wendy Richards mom and dad were local to the area, Dolly, her mom came from Devonshire St and her dad George, from Talbot St, they met, courted and were married in 1937, they were wed at St Chrysostoms, where later on Wendy was to be Christened in the March of 1944, Wendy told me of the cost for two cars for the wedding and they came to the grand sum of £2, and of the wedding ring it cost the vast amount of £1.9 shillings! After were to make their home in Allens Rd, George served as a gunner in the RAF from 1939 to 1945, and served in France, Germany, Holland and Belgium. Wendy came along in 1944, and was born in Dudley Rd Hospital and grew in the Bacchus Rd area. Their house was one of the usual types up the street, no bathrooms of course, if it wasn't the tin bath as I've said, it was the washing baths in Bacchus Rd, the front door ran straight off the pavement, nothing of a front garden, only a back yard to play in, or the street. The road had one shop and that was in the middle ran by a Mrs Parker, this, as many other shops were a major convenience, this shopkeeper would even sell half a loaf, a single rasher of bacon and even a couple of eggs!

Names of families came flooding back such as the Bonners, Such's, Potters, Nortons, Bakers and the Pritchards, Mrs Pritchard was a bus conductress, and of their children Wendy went to Benson Rd School with Sandra and Pat Bonner, Dianne Norton, Jean and Barbara Baker, Carole Pritchard, Linda Emery and others such as Wynford Davies, Regina Dudley and Annette Colley.

Later Wendy was to meet a mate of mine, Bob Levy from up our street, and settle down to married life in Perrot St. I had grown up with Bob, played together, went to the same schools and in later years worked at the same bakery, Scribbans', I left and went on the 'Pop, with Mason's whilst Bob went to Bradfords and to this day still works there. They are also great friends of ours and see each other as often as we can, but invariably go back in time and talk of the old times. That's what memories are all about.

Wendy and Bob Levy on the right
me and our 'Marg' on the left in our younger days
(R Levy)

51

BENSON ROAD, FROM SCHOOL GATES TO SETTENS

In the history of Winson Green, roads and streets changed their names like the weather. From the continuation of Bacchus Lane, Soho Rd made it's way down towards the cross-roads of Lodge Rd and down towards Boulton's Manufactory. We know now that these names changed over the years Bacchus Lane became a road, Soho changed to Benson, and of course Lodge became Park Rd.

So to all the people who lived in Benson Rd they were unique in knowing their name was purloined to move to the top of St Michael's Hill. It is only a short road from a split with Bacchus Rd. Harding and Talbot Streets came from the right and a bit further down Allen's Rd was divided in two.

It is best remembered for the school, but was home to Setten and Derwards, which I shall describe later on in this chapter.

It was a busy road, and a noisy one at that as the main railway line from Wolverhampton ran through a bridge under the road towards the top of the hill. There would be a variety of trains, from goods to local services. Expresses would blow their whistles as they hurtled through Soho station making their way to Snow Hill. It was a popular station and many excursions and day trips were to make their way from those platforms, not just to the seaside, but like I did, fishing trips to the Severn Valley. It closed down after the Beeching days and left dormant. It seemed that it would never open again for passengers, but that was all to change when the Midland Metro was opened between Birmingham and Wolverhampton, also the line was extended from the bottom of Queenshead Rd and The Black Patch park for passengers on British Rail. Up until that time it was freight only. Only now it was to be the new Snowhill Station that we would arrive at, it isn't the same but its great to see the line being used again for passenger use. When I was young I would stand at the bottom of Perrot St to watch all sorts of locomotives go through, Castles, Kings, Manors and the usual pannier tanker, which we knew as 'Matchboxes', I didn't use this station though as you had to buy a platform ticket (one penny!) I could use that to buy a gob stopper or two.

The area was bereft though for public transport, apart from the 96 and the

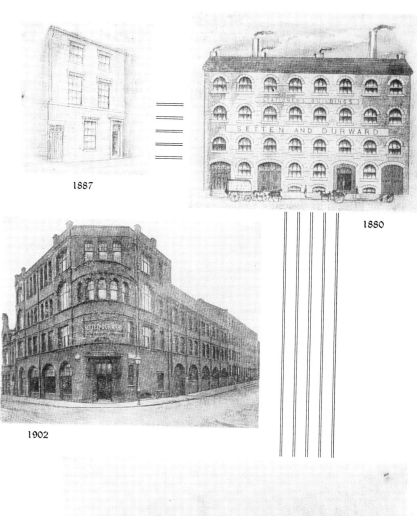

1887

1880

1902

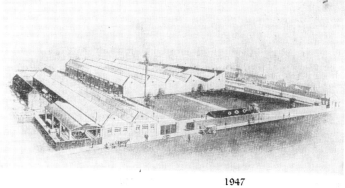

1947

53

Setten & Durward Ltd.

request the pleasure of your company

at a

Dinner & Dance

to Celebrate the 70th Anniversary
of the establishment of the Firm

to be held at the

Old Crown & Cushion Hotel

Birchfield Road, Perry Barr

on

Thursday, September 25th 1947

6-30 for 7-0

Miss L. Bamford,

Dancing 8-30 to 12-30   R.S.V.P.

54

number 11, there were none around the Park Rd area, up and around that part of Handsworth and also down to Hockley, so no wonder people worked, shopped and drank locally.

This street contained the usual shops together side by side with small to large factories, interspersed with dwellings, and the usual back houses, After Bacchus Rd, which was mostly residential interspersed with small shops, industry came in earnest towards Factory Rd, the largest was Setten and Derwards they produced everything for the stationary trade, the most notable was I X L files, which are still used today, they made all sorts of sundries from mathematical instruments, ink stands, letter files and cash boxes, it was a large employer, mostly of women from the area, because of the nature of the work entailed. The history of the firm started in 1877 in the town, it moved after a short while to bigger premises in 1880, in 1902 they were to move to Livery St, this wasn't to be the last as they moved out of the city to Benson Rd. Therein in 1947 they were to hold their centenary as the illustration shows, it was to close its doors in the 1960's. To those who worked there it will bring back many memories, some happy, some sad because of the closure of a firm that gave many a job in the area, and the loss of a pal or two.

January 1962, Setten and Derwards Christmas Party
Ted and Maureen Rudge's daughter Susan seated
next to the lady serving.
(T Rudge)

There were a few other small factories, Frank Dudley who made washers, R G Boardman, tools, Russons the plumbers and a grand sounding name of Corinthian Products Ltd who were sheet metal workers. Shops were of the usual, there was Percy Taylor who kept the florists, Isabella Tyler who owned the local greengrocers, Bill Yeomans the butcher and a number of little grocers, Selina Cox, Lucy Parsons, Sid Bailey and Irene Lewis, a ladies hairdressers known as Beryl's, but the one shop that I remember from knocking around that area with an old pal Colin Muddiford, was Perkes and Son who kept the bakers shop just inside Benson Rd. The smell of the bread and the cakes in the window lives on for ever. In later years I was to know the son as he used to go to the Ninevah dance hall, he was older than me as he had done National Service in the R A F.

At the top of the street, we start at the railway station. Just inside Talbot St, there stands the Wonder Vaults, even though the area has been redeveloped the pub still stands today. If it could speak it could tell of many tales I'm sure, the area abounded with pubs and were always well supported, but we'll meet more in our story.

I've always described in any of my stories of school days, teachers who made an impression on us and schools that we went to for the first time. Benson Rd wasn't any different, the school was in the main catchment area for the local population, who after would go to Handsworth New Rd. The school is still open today and people who lived and went to that school would never forget their teachers, I tried to keep times in order but I found that the amount of information sent to me on the school varied over the years and some teachers were to teach others in later years, so I hope the reader will bear with me.

The school was built in 1902. This was to be an infant and junior school and was to be a feeder school for children who after the age of eleven would either go on to secondary or grammar schools. Most of the children who didn't pass for the grammar went to Handsworth New Road. The school stands halfway down Benson Rd on the left hand side. Now let's find out some more of the kids and teachers.

Barbara Boscott who now lives in Bournville came from Bacchus Rd and went to Benson Rd School in the early fifties, the school hadn't changed much as that the infants shared their playground, but the juniors were segregated. Even though her memories of where she grew up are with clarity, no more so than the school and it's teachers that they were to make an impression on her, there was a Miss Dumelow, who taught second top class, she was her favourite, Miss Dumelow would be met by Barbara and other children on the corner of Talbot St by the train station, and would walk with her down to the school. She would give children in her class sweets. They would go out of the school for drawing lessons with board and easels, invariably it would be by the side of the railway, Barbara's favourite was the signal box.

Another teacher was a Miss Shiner, she was very strict, all the children were all frightened of her, she taught needlework, if a child couldn't tie a neat knot in a needle with the cotton she couldn't start sewing, needless to say Barbara wasn't always successful and she never learned to sew!

It wasn't just the school which remains in her memory. Like all of us it's a jumble, but one spark and it all ignites, even to the caretakers at the school Mr and Mrs Jones with their son Bobby. School friends became a way of life to all of us, long cherished, promises of friendship forever, and now just names, like Roy Poyner who lived in Park Rd, Margaret Ward out of Dover St, Cliff Nurrish who lived in Musgrave Rd, now there is the light going on in my memory, I went to school at Handsworth New Rd as we all know, and lo and behold it was of the same family, my mate was Paul Nurrish, at the time our dad worked backstage at the Hippodrome, and during the 50's up and coming Rock and Roll artists were making their names, I was lucky as our dad would get me complimentary tickets for the matinees of these shows, and Paul and I would go to see them, he was a full blown 'Ted' even at school, and wore all the drapes when out, we left school and went our different ways, but many years later when working on my own I met up with one of his brothers in Burntwood, Staffordshire, but that is another story.

Another young wench that came from that area was Hilda Fry, previously Walcroft, her friends Mary Bubb from Benson Rd and Pauline Jeavons out of Devonshire, her mom and dad kept the fish and chip shop there and Hilda helped to prepare the chips, she would cut up the newspapers ready for use, and all for the grand sum of sixpence and a bag of chips! a labour of love. There were others who went to Benson Rd schools, with the Walcroft sisters, Hilda, as we know, Brenda, Phyliss and Doris, the latter from 1932 to 1938 and a progression of years to Hilda from 1942 to 1947. They lived at number 3 Railway Cottages. Little insignificant things like washing the silver tops off the bottles of milk which were given out to the children, and threading coloured wool to make purses and bags.

Though not all the time were of the happiest, during a short time whilst Hilda was in hospital, one the teachers, Miss Shiner would come and visit her, there was a double reason for this as she would bring in school work

Hilda Fry second from right with Mother and Family X'mas 1958
(H Fry)

Hilda's wedding in 1968
at St Chrysostoms
(H Fry)

as in the perchance Hilda wouldn't fall behind.

The family travels took them from Railway Cottages to Radnor St and finally to 304 Park Rd. Hilda later married Eric Fry at St Chrystostems in 1968, and the officiating officer was no less the Rev A J Hartley (was this the famous author on fishing?). They now live out at Rednal, what a difference, you don't hear the birds cough out there!

Another pupil of later years was Janice Smith, she was at Benson Rd Juniors between 1963 and 1967. The Head Mistress then was Miss Legge, the school secretary was a Mrs Fisher. The teachers from the first year were Mr Evans, second Miss Edwards, third was a Mr Sheen and the last teacher was Miss Neal, her named changed in that last year as she got married and went to a Mrs Shaw. Other teachers' names spring to mind with Mr Phillips and Miss Millard who taught other classes in the juniors. The school is still there and still very active. Other teachers were to come and go as the same with pupils and the memories of Barbara and Janice and the likes of many a child through the years have not dimmed their memories of school friends and teachers no matter how hard their schooling was.

Infant children in class
(D Thomas)

This is not all of Benson Rd but just a reminder of some that lived in and around this area, Peter Hill who is in his late 60's went to Benson Rd schools,. His memory now fails him with names but he remembers a teacher by the name of Mrs Green, and the Bubb's from out of Benson Rd, (it must have been a big family as I keep coming across this name) after that he went to Handsworth New Rd, All of us knew of our teachers at that school, and of those who taught there before I went, but the one he remembered was 'Jammy' Hartley, and 'Slinky' Priest. Their reputations certainly preceded them.

Peter lived in Factory Rd, opposite Cheneys, he remembers a shop that he went to as a child, it was Beresfords on the corner of Queens Avenue. As a young lad he would fetch the usual jug of ale for his dad from the Black Horse. His dad was a member of the Ninevah Rd Working mens Club, and later followed in his footsteps. A family friend by the name of Tommy Harper kept a garage and taxi firm in Benson Rd. Peter was one of those who had associations with the 'Flat' as his dad was the manager of Marsh and Baxters, he came to the 'Flat' after his branch in Smallbrook St was bombed. His wife Brenda also had an association with the same shopping centre, as her dad, George Lowe owned the Hardware shop on the 'Flat'. it was later sold, and the new owners Gaylors, sold glass and mirrors. So all of us has got a story, if not a tale to tell.

We're now down at the cross roads, with Handsworth straight ahead and Park Rd crossing in front, this is the road where we are heading for, left to Handsworth and right to Hockley, let's start from the Ninevah Rd end and make our way along this long and winding road to the 'Flat'.

PARK ROAD FROM THE NINEVAH TO FACTORY ROAD

I'm splitting up this piece for reasons of the vast amount information that was given to me, It would have been unfair to have crammed it all into one solitary chapter. So now we go on our travels from Handsworth all the way down into Hockley and find the shops, pubs, businesses and most importantly the people.

From open countryside at the bottom end of Park Rd would start a ribbon of houses that would stretch all the way up into the town. Parcels of land were bought and developed piecemeal, railways dissected the area, the skyline altered from open fields to viaducts, houses, factories and a multitude of roads and streets providing housing for the needs of another working class area. Park Rd was one sided after going round the bend towards Musgrave Rd, then an open field till coming towards the 'Flat' opposite Dover St. It must have been a grand setting when the grounds and pools of the Boulton estate were there, after the pools had been filled in and the area was traversed by railway lines the name of the road was kept, it was a bit of a misnomer.

Even though the 'Flat' was a veritable magnet for shopping, the cross roads with factory Rd, Benson Rd and Park Rd had its own shopping area. Naturally it was for the locals, but as well for the factories in the district, and not forgetting of course the workers from Cheneys in Factory Rd. A sign that it was well represented for shoppers that there was a Wrenson's grocery store in this part of Park Rd, though others were to make a living. Coming up from the bottom end by the railway arches on the left hand side was Walls the ice cream makers, next door the tea manufacturers Brooke Bonds, next came a scrap metal merchants by the name of C H Ford and Co, then a little grocers ran by Mrs Wickes. We now meet the first of the pubs in Park Rd, it was the Old Engine, not a large establishment but frequently used, next door was Nicholls the boot and shoe repairer. Before the corner of Factory Rd was a business that sold vans, it's slogan was 'A Man for a Van' (of these two businesses, we shall talk later). Over the road before the cross-roads were met coming up from Bacchus Rd was a Garage owned by a couple of brothers by the name of Garratt, then houses, followed by Russon the plumbers on the corner of Berry St, on the other side of the street was Collins the builders, before this was

Jacksons the coal merchants. There was a big yard between the next block of houses, then Johnson's the green grocers. We're now up to Benson Rd. On the other corner on this side of the road was Wrensons the grocers followed by a butcher, Robertson's, would you believe in our modern upfront society in the name of our next shop, Leonard Cox 'Fancy Drapers' skeins of wool of all different gauges and cottons of all descriptions. If a bet was required it was to be Bill Tibbit's, turf accountants, another green grocers, Crockers, and following yet by another butchers by the name of Featherstone's. Then came the highlight of any night, the proverbial fish and chip shop. I myself remember this well, when I was only a kid I knocked about with a mate who lived in Benson Rd and we used to go to this particular establishment. It was the only shop that I knew that sold 'batters' for a penny a bag . I didn't remember the name till I started writing this book, but when I was told it came back to me, it was Bennetts. After this was Newtown Body Repairs, another grocers, Moore and Sons, then at the corner of Musgrave Rd was Parkes the timber merchants. Then came St Chrisostoms, Dover St came next, on the other corner was another pub, the Old Mint Tavern.

Coming back on ourselves. from the corner of Factory Rd towards the 'Flat' was, and is the Soho Tavern, Howells the newsagent came next, a resplendent name of a block of terraced houses came after, Park Grove, yet another grocers by the name of Noakes, then Doris Hale who kept a drapers shop followed by another row of terraced houses known as Church Grove. After these houses was another shop which I can't find out what they sold, all I know the name was Taylor. (No doubt someone will tell me!) No more houses or buildings came into view till we came towards the 'Flat' Now it's time to meet a one time local.

Ray Clarke, was just one of many who were to live in the area. He has his own memories of living and working in this part of Park Rd.

He wasn't born and bred in our area, but took to it, and would never forget it. He was born in Acocks Green and his association with Winson Green began when he came out of the army and went for a job at Lucas's. He had to report to the receptionist, whom he took a liking to, and before long they were going out. His wife to be, Maureen, came from Kings Heath. Eventually they got married, and the need for somewhere to live was paramount, Maureen worked with a girl called Jean Wardle whose father was a landlord with properties in Park Rd. This is where they started their married life. It was to be 422 Park Rd on the cross-roads of

*Looking over towards Handsworth and Smethwick
from Bacchus Rd across the Great Western Railway
(B Boscott)*

Factory, Benson and Park Rd. It was the usual terraced house which went straight off the street into the parlour. To live in that little area was no mean feat. Other people have remarked about the noise of the railway goods yard shunting at all times of the day. He will never forget the clanking and banging that went on when trucks were coupled up to one another, visitors would come to see them and would be visibly shocked upon seeing teacups shaking as another train was making up its required amount of trucks, bang, bang, bang. It was always the same question "how can you live with that noise all the time?" Well like all the rest they had to, till something came up and they'd move, but that wasn't the end to the sound of steam engines. Up Benson Rd the main Great Western line ran under the bridge and trains would sound their whistle when passing the station at the top of Talbot St. It was a fact that over the years as people moved out of similar places to live somewhere quieter they couldn't get used to not having noise around them. It would be the case of getting used to the quiet rather than a constant noise all the time. Ray had a job at Cheneys but after a couple of years had the sack. He had other jobs but after 18 months he heard that the foreman who gave him the sack had died so on trying his luck he went back and asked if he could have his job back. The firm said they would give him another chance and he was grateful to them. Times were hard and every penny coming in the house was needed. His wife Maureen cleaned over the other side of the road at the

Soho Tavern. She even took their little lad in a pram with her. Times were hard and on one occasion he had to use a commemorative five shilling piece that he had been given for the Coronation. He duly went into Wrensons to see the manager and asked if it was legal tender, upon being told yes, the groceries were paid for. That was the end of his five bob piece and possibly his son's inheritance at that time. On another occasion the rent was due that afternoon at four o'clock and having no money he went over the road to Mr Nicholls the shoe repairer, he was the only man he knew well over this side of town, telling him of his plight Mr Nicholls opened the till and took out a ten shilling note. That was the rent for the week, he thought a lot of him and they were to become friends for many years to come. Shopping was done locally for Ray and his wife at most of the shops which I have mentioned. Jackson's the coal merchants lived close, by separated by a big yard where he kept his lorry and his German Heinkel bubble car. They had a son by the name of Roy whom they looked after when his parents went out, and to this day they are still in contact. As time went on they moved back across the city, but the comradeship that they got from this working class suburb was never to be found again for them. They knew their neighbours and their strengths, everyone was the same, no airs and graces. Admittedly their new home was much more pleasant, and they had a front garden but the neighbours weren't the same. On a lighter note, people can give a wrong impression in other peoples mind. On the other side of the road next to the shoe repair shop was a little company that used to sell vehicles. As I said earlier on it was called 'A Man for a Van'. Well one of the brothers always had his trilby on at the back of his head, and Ray always felt he looked and sounded like a 'Spiv' and he wouldn't buy one off him, He was probably far away from the truth but wouldn't admit it. His love of motorbikes and fishing were his pastimes and he is now a well known figure on the River Avon at Eckington, a long way from the 'cut' to the jewel of Warwickshire rivers.

We'll finish with this part of Park Rd with me going back to Nicholls the shoe repairers. He had a daughter who had long blonde hair set in a pony-tail. Well, I used to go round and see my mate from out of Benson Rd, and like all young lads do, a heart starts to flutter, she was lovely, but I think, being tall and gangly with a slight stammer I never stood a chance, Ah well! that's love's young dreams. Mind you I think I was about thirteen at the time!

Let's now traipse the remainder of this long and distinguished road.

Roy Jackson in a car of the time 'A Three Wheel Bubble Car'
(R Clarke)

Ray Clarke's son with his dad's helmet on
(R Clarke)

65

STILL IN PARK ROAD BUT ONWARDS TO THE 'FLAT'

I have gone to the end of the area in the first part of this chapter from the railway bridge at the bottom of Bacchus Rd and Park Rd, over the cross-roads leading one way towards Lodge Rd and the other way to St Michael's Hill, we now have come round the left hand bend to Musgrave Rd

St Chrysostoms, what a mouthful! It must have been for any young child going to Sunday school for the first time. The church was built in the latter part of the 19th century on a grand design as was All Saints and Bishop Latimers. It was the main church within its own parish, like Bishop Latimers. Maureen Greensall's grandparents were from Ladywood, the Wallis's were married there in 1902, and a copy of the marriage lines shown on this page has a delightful engraving of the church at that time.

Following on from there we come to Dover St. Between this and Norton St were mainly houses with a pub on both corners. They were like book-ends, the one on the corner of Dover St was the Old Mint Tavern and the opposite on the corner of Norton St was the Railway Tavern. Park Rd went straight on towards the 'Flat' and Norton St to the right, at this juncture of the road Wharf St ran off on a diagonal. This was probably amongst one the oldest streets in the area. It led to the wharf at the basin of the canal.

All Saints Church, All Saints St
(J Landon)

The Railway Tavern, corner of Norton St and Park Rd
(J Landon)

This wharf was at the end of a spur from the 'Old Canal' which was built in the 1700's. It was the closest of points to serve Boulton's new works. It would have been horse drawn from the narrow boats and vice versa. Coal and materials the one way and the finished article the other, the canal might have been slower but it saved on the costs in going along toll roads. It must have looked and seemed idyllic in those days. This wasn't always to be as the area grew and houses and businesses filled in the surrounding district. Other streets were to be renamed but Wharf St kept its own.

The street mostly contained houses to the right hand side running up to the wharf, Bill Green who lived in Wharf St at number 1 Millsboro Place remembers Leonard Leigh's, one of the two business's in the street, and seems to think that after they moved over to the Perry Barr area they became Leigh Environmental, the waste disposal firm. The other business was Walkers Transport at the bottom end of the street. It backed onto Bradfords Bakery which was in Norton St.

There was one shop he remembers at this time. It was in Wharf St and that was Hetteys, previously Stantons, a public house, there were quite a few rooms over this establishment. It was, as the story goes an early B and B for the boat men who had made their way to the wharf. This would sound plausible as traffic on the canals up to the war was still in demand.

During the war storage of aluminium was held at Leighs and as kids do they mooched around the canal and came across loads of metal. Upon which a quick and sharp, "Clear off", from one of the workers would soon send them on their way. He wondered why all this stuff was kept there, but soon lost interest and found something else up the canal to do.

At the end of Wharf St was an alley which came at the top end of Wharf Lane. It was only a small street, about a hundred and fifty yards in length, and it was always assumed that at one time this building in the middle of the lane, which had been derelict for some time, had been a blacksmiths, and naturally a place for the shoeing of the horses for the canal trade.

At the bottom end of the lane is Park Rd, on the left hand corner was Jefferson's the grocers and on the right hand, Wilkes's newsagents and drapery shop. To those people who once resided in this small and insignificant street what a wondrous picture it would have made a couple of hundred years before. Like all the rest Bill Green moved away but kept his memories.

Park Road down towards 'The Flat'
(circa 1960)

Sadly we are now out of Winson Green proper, and find ourselves in Hockley, I don't want to tread on any one else's toes, but as I've gone this far I'm now going to continue on this last little bit of Park Rd.

Down towards Abbey St like the rest of any other part of a growing city houses and factories would exist side by side, after Wilkes's newsagents. Factories such as E W Richards and Son and Foundryflux Ltd who made foundry requisites. In between these two factories houses and the occasional small shop would exist. On the other side of Abbey St coming down to Goode St was Mrs Thortons a confectioner (was this the fore runner of the famous Thorntons chocolate shops?) and a capstan manufactory. Griffiths, Gilbert, Lloyd and Co came next, before one of the last of the general shops then we meet the 'Flat' with Mrs Kelly's. Crossing Goode St was a newsagents ran by Jennie Weston. It was the only business on this side of the road, apart from the Royal Exchange, an Atkinsons public house at the bottom of Park Rd.

From the other side of the road from Wharf Lane were a row of houses and small business's whose gardens and workshops backed onto Hockley Pool railway sidings. Going down along this row of buildings were such business's as F McCabe an off-licence, Olds the Builders, Sentio Press a printers, J J Blacks the bookie, a painter and decorator W O'Connor, and another beer retailer Mrs Waller. Two grand sounding names for two rows of houses, Victoria Avenue and Henwick Place came after, in between these houses and Orford Rd was a small cul-de-sac with Mrs Clintons a drapers and Mrs Rabone a general shopkeeper. Further on down more factories were to be found, small and large towards Whitmore St. These included W J Eyre Turned Parts Ltd, S H Electrical, Midland Drawing Office, Perry and Walker electro platers, not just factories though there were the usual shops Elsie Smith a newsagent, William Gray who owned a drapers. On the corner of Whitmore St were dining rooms run by a C Doyle, handy for the number of factory and office staff in the area for lunchtime breaks. On the other side of the Street was the Erdington Laundry Co, next door was Jacksons the turf accountants, then Sam Taylor a well known barber and next door Joan's the ladies hairdresser, Mrs Blanche Evans with her fish a chip shop, and yet another dining rooms this time owned and run by F Mason, I've tried to include as many of the shops and businesses in the district as I could, but if there are a few that I have missed I'm sorry. I hope what I have written will bring a few memories back to those who lived down this end of Park Rd.

I haven't finished yet though, I had heard from a number of people from the 'London Buildings' and this intrigued me and I wanted to find out more and the answer came through our next local to the area.

Looking up to London Buildings
(circa 1960)

Chas Farrington, whom I'm indebted to, gave me an extract from his time in being born and bred in Park Rd. These buildings, where he lived though were unique as they had a room underneath the groundfloor front room which was entered by steps running from the street. Where the term London buildings came from is anyones guess? They could have been the style in a city for the want of more rooms to a building, if it did mean living below ground floor level, Chas lived at one time at 2 back of 89 and at 1 back of 87. These houses were back to back, unlike other back to backs which were usually built up an entry or a court, these were on the street. Normal looking terrace type houses, they were joined to the one on the front. After a time his family moved round the corner into Whitmore St.

Park Rd with Whitmore St to the right in the 1950s
(J Landon)

He was born in the mean and lean 30's, even up to the early 60's it was still to be a busy and industrious area, but in those early years times for him and the like were hard as in all similar working class districts. Growing up a rigid social distinction even in those times, there was a division by which house you lived in, from a back to back to a villa type on the street

71

with a front and back door. Chas was to be one of the former but that did-n't stop him from feeling he was as good as any one else. The usual schools would be attended in the area from infant, junior and seniors, he remembers the fortunate or unfortunate, as he said for those that passed for the grammar schools, they were taunted and ragged something rotten.

Pleasures for him and his mates growing up in Lodge Rd area on a Saturday afternoon were spent in the "twopenny crush" at the Palladium on Hockley Brook or at the local library at Springhill. Mercifully the build-ing has been left alone to this present day in its original form. On a Saturday night the highlight was going to the local chippie for a twopen-ny fish and a "pennorth" of chips (in old money of course!), swigging from a bottle of beer which was fetched from the local outdoor, in those days up to the fifties, a sticker was put over the stopper of the bottle to stop any beer from being drunk till getting it home to the elders. It didn't stop him though from having a swig! Train spotting up at the yard at Hockley, watching the blacksmith shoeing horses in Whitmore St, or helping the brass founder in his back shed, this was all about growing up and learn-ing the real facts in life, going to the pawn shop on a Monday morning, listening, if at home, to neighbours gossiping and talking of their opera-tions and diseases, and the saying of the women who had "had it all taken away" being the local saying for a Hysterectomy. Living in Hockley was his life and after leaving school he worked at Lucas's for 42 years. He also played in jazz bands as a banjo player. I add this post script which I think sums up what a lot of us must think, if not say. These are his words.

"There used to be a local song called " I can't find Brummagem". Well there should be one called " I can't find Hockley" with the disappearance of those old pubs. The Abbey pub (known as the Wrecksome) The Brown Lion, The Benyon, The Turks Head, The Watt Tavern, The Great Western, The Hydraulic, The Exchange and so many more.

"Were they good or bad old days? I'll tell you what I think, they were mean, petty, poor, bloody awful but magnificent"

Of memories of Park Rd at this end I was indebted to others who gave me an insight to the area. Such as Robert Gould who lived down the bottom end. He was born and bred in the area, and went to Icknield St Schools' where he was taught by Mr Wise, Mr Benson and the grand sounding name Mr Warwick Smith. The head was a Mr Fleet Robert later played football for Hockley Celtic in the Sunday league.

The Welcome Tavern 'Little' Park Road
(J Landon)

It was a hive of activity, his friends (some of whom he still keeps in contact with to this day) were to get up to all the usual habits and recreations as of all those from that area. Train spotting at All Saints, swimming in the 'cut' at the 'loop' at Winson Green, watching the buses at the depot in Ford St, and at the wharf at Soho pool, all these were adventure parks (if they didn't catch you). One of his friends was Bob Yates, he was one of five, the eldest, Jack, was to die at Scapa Flow on the Royal Oak, which was torpedoed at the outbreak of war, others were Bob alias 'Yacka', who was one of his five mates and still friends to this day, the others were Roy 'Jacko' Jackson, 'Nobby Richards, Alan 'Bona' Jones, and 'Blackie'. Even he had a nickname it was 'Bibby' Gould. Over the road from Goode St was Sterns who sold ice-cream, toffee apples and Sunday papers! On bonfire nights the area where we played 'Polly on the mop stick' was the attic highs the backa's. The Mecca, a double Knack where we went up one entry and down the other with chalk marks across the road when we played 'Copper on the Bridge'. Growing older, pubs were to come to the fore such as the Royal Exchange which only sold beer, no spirits, and The Abbey

Vaults where a good sing song could be had on a Saturday night in the little lounge bar,

The shops, pubs and factories I shan't describe again as they are all too familiar to all of those from that one particular place but the one shop intrigued me when told was a barbers who put a sign up in the window when he was called up to serve his country- GONE TO FIGHT THE GERMANS, which remained there for quite a few years.

Bob lived at 4 back of 102 and didn't move very far. When he got married in 1951 he went to live at the back of 104, Mr Ryder who had lived at this house left them the fowl pen and six eggbound chickens! People say you should never look back, but Bob has and is still enjoying it, as in Roland in our next story.

Like all the rest their stories are hard but fair, an understanding of what an area can bring out in people, times never change, only the people.

Let's go back even further to the 1920's. This is a small piece on another resident from this little part of the world. Roland Smith was born in Carver St in 1926, four years later the family moved to 251 Park Rd, which today is one of the very few original houses still standing. Moving was also a trial as there wasn't enough room in the van and he had to make his way with his mother by foot, carrying the family pet, a cat, in a sack! His first impressions were of what a marvellous house. It had a long back garden which backed onto Soho Pool wharf, and it was a joy to watch the trains shunting. When he was ready to go to school it was not to be All Saints, where his other brothers and sisters had attended, but to St Pauls in the Jewellery quarter on his parents insistence. For the fare of one halfpenny he caught the 32 tram from outside Scribbans' bakery to Chamberlains clock at the top of Warstone Lane. This he did till he was 14. Scribbans' bakery would follow him through his youth, and when he grew older he started courting his wife to be. She was the daughter of one of the employees, Harry Pittaway, was a night shift worker at the bakery. The building was a landmark, impressive on the corner of Goode St and Lodge Rd, with a tower rising above the building completed ornately with a dome. On the other corner we all remember the Hydraulic public house. Well Roland at the ripe old age of 22, and his wife held their wedding reception there. Roland and his Betty were to have one son, and he was christened at All Saints, their lives would revolve around this area with all the memories as others, till eventually they would move on and others would fill their places.

We're nearly there, our goal, the 'Flat' beckons us, but let's be a little more patient.

Pentecostal Church on the 'Flat'
Vic Jones

GETTING ALL DRESSED UP TO GO OUT DANCING

For this chapter, I would like to thank Laurie Hornsby for the help given to me. He has written a book on the Birmingham rock scene titled 'Brum Rocked' and the information he allowed me to use was indispensable. For all of us who grew up in this area during the 50's and 60's, I hope it brings back some memories.

To all of us kids the thought of going out on a Saturday night to a dance hall, was the highlight of the week. Well it was for me. I would come home from the bakery, have some tea, and start to get ready. A newly laundered shirt, all crisp and inviting, my best suit coming out of the wardrobe, and thinking to myself "I wish our mom didn't put those moth balls in there". A smart pair of shoes, and a brand new tie that I had bought from Groom's the same afternoon. That place was a Mecca for the teenage lads who lived and worked around the bottom of Windmill Lane, Smethwick. Then the ceremonial combing of the hair, it would take ages till it came just right, and off I would go. I'd go down the bottom of the yard and wait for my mates. First would be Roy Richards then Jeff Hughes. We'd make our way up Foundry Rd into Handsworth New Rd and meet up with Bob Dolman. The night was full of anticipation, we'd got a few bob in our pockets, and we looked the bees knees. Down Handsworth New Rd and into Ninevah Rd, and then up Bacchus Rd to the Ninevah Dance Studios. I think we paid 2/- to get in. Up the stairs we'd go and into the dance. Saturday night was rock and roll night. During the week it was mostly strict tempo for learners and medallists, as well as devising a ballroom version of rock and roll, it never caught on as us teenagers wanted to do our own 'thing' and on a Saturday night slowly but surely the purists were to be driven out, and rock and roll came to the fore. At a given time there would be an interval, some would buy soft drinks, but the more adventurous would go down to the pub in Bacchus Rd. I was a tall lad and I could get away with looking over 18 when I was only 16! Not very clever I think to myself today, but I suppose that in my mind it was what growing up was all about. Chancing our arm springs to mind! Three halves of mild and no girl were safe. Then back into the dance. If the owner of the studio didn't smell your breath first.

Unlike today when a dance doesn't finish till the early hours of the morning, at 11 o'clock it was all over. You either clicked and you walked a girl home, with the hope of a snog and date for the Regal Picture House the following afternoon. Or the long walk back home with your mates and think of better luck the following week.

The dress would alter beyond all recognition. Gone were the suits that would be worn in the winter and flannels and sports jackets in the summer for the men and twin sets for the women. Rock and Roll changed all that. Not everybody was a teddy boy or girl, though narrow bottoms were to be the norm, girls wore layers of tulle under wide skirts and a small scarf around the neck, stiletto heels or flat soled shoes (strictly for bopping in) were to be the fashion. The hair styles changed. Boys copied the American actor Tony Curtis with a difference, the back of the hair was shaped into what was known as the 'ducks arse' or the D A for short. Girls wore their hair in the pony tail style others straight with a kiss curl. The era of the teddy boy didn't last that long but the mould had been broken. In the early 60's the long drape coats, drainpipe trousers and crepe soled shoes, gave way to the new Italian style, much shorter jackets with four or more buttons, trousers that tapered down and the inevitable 'winkle pickers'. Girls were to change their dress as well, pencil skirts took over from the voluminous wider variety, even the shoes were to change, stilettos were still in but more fashionable, different shades of colours which followed the same style of the men with pointed toes. Hair styles changed as well, it was to be the start of the bouffant, more so than the beehive with loads of lacquer. From the mass of hair of the teddy boy era young mens styles were to change as well, it was to be the razor cut, short hair that copied the clothes, even though the hair was still to be cut into the 'Boston' at the nape of the neck. This was the time that I thought was the smartest, as the 60's went on clothes began to change once again when the mods and Rockers came on the scene. Later on narrow bottoms gave way to the flares, but that was to be in the future for someone else to reminisce about.

The Ninevah dance studio was for records only, as was Laura Dixons in the town and Hawleys on the Dudley Rd. These studios were a start for a majority of teenagers who wanted to learn how to dance. Apart from these studios there were church halls that had regular Saturday night dances.

Abruptly the Ninevah Dance Studio closed. A van ran into Broadmead's the television shop which was directly underneath the studio, unfortunately the building was classed unstable and pulled down. George and Dorothy Carless attempted to keep the name going, they hired other halls in the area, one was in Oxhill Rd at the top of Grove Lane, and one just off the Holyhead Rd towards Highland Rd. It was not to be the same and the old gang finally split up. It was such a shame as I am sure if it hadn't have been for the accident in the first place this particular venue would have been a Mecca for future dancers for many years to come.

As I've always said picture houses were for the weekdays, but Saturday nights were for going out, all dressed up and to go out dancing, it was all a part of growing up. Up the Green Pat Dimmock and her pals would go to the Woodcraft by Summerfield Park with her mates. It was a youth club, and that's where she learned to rock and roll, then it was over to something more salubrious, Hawley's Dance Studio, but the Tower at Edgbaston 'Rezza' became the place to go for those up that end of the Green. The mood of the times were changing, The big bands were still around, but it needed something special, for our generation. We wanted more from the regular dance tunes, Bill Haley and Elvis Presley altered all that and it was never to be the same again.

Over the other side of the Atlantic this new and weird and wonderful sound came. The legends would always stick with us, Fats Domino, Chuck Berry, Buddy Holly and the Crickets, the Everley Brothers and many more too numerous to mention. Back home though we had our own home grown talent Tommy Steele, Billy Fury, Cliff Richard, Marty Wilde, Joe Brown and so on. It was now to be rock and roll and things changed. Early television shows such as 'Six five Special' and 'Oh Boy' were the pace setters, and young men and women wanted to copy their idols with their interpretations of this new phenomenon. It started with skiffle, with artists such as Lonnie Donnegan, The Vipers, Chas Macdevit and Nancy Whisky, to improvise out came the proverbial wash board, tea chest with a broomstale and string, a couple of budding guitarists, who bought them on the never never. The washboard and tea chest went and in came a set of drums and electric guitars to take over. This now was to be the age of the groups. Modelling themselves on their idols, now their big chance came.

There were still the crooners and big band singers, over here we had Ronnie Hilton, Dickie Valentine who were the ones that we would smooch to on the dance floor. The big band era was slowly passing away with the likes of Ted Heath and Joe Loss, it was still the era of the bands but with a difference.

Up and coming groups would make their names known amongst the dance halls around the city. In our area during the late 50's the old Rookery cinema was bought by a couple by the name of Regan, a strict tempo couple who had vision, and changed it into a dance hall. It was to be known as the Plaza, this was the new Mecca for dancers in the Handsworth area, at the same time was to open another Plaza in Old Hill in the Black Country. This pair knew that teenagers wanted more than just a dancehall, with the same group week in week out, but visiting groups as well. Not only was there to be a big band but a regular backing group. Most famous at Handsworth were the Beachcombers. Over the years they backed most of the top singers of the day who visited the Plaza, In their own right they became recording artists for no less a name than Norrie Paramour. One of the group came out of Willis Rd by the name of John Ship. (The Green has scored again) The big band era was still there but it needed something more, and rock and roll groups filled the spot. At the Locarno in Hurst St, the stage revolved round. One side a band would play for a spell and then revolve to a group, at this time it would have been Mike Sheridan and the Night Riders. This was a new innovation, not all dance halls had this provision, but it didn't take anything away from the rest. At the baths in Thimblemill Rd Ronnie Hancox and his band played, his lead singer was Susan Maughan. At the Gay Tower in Edgbaston, El Riot and the Rebels fronted the resident band, as just over the border at the Coliseum on Bearwood Rd rock and roll was provided by the Deltas and back down the town Gerry Levene and his Night Riders played at the West End. Not all venues stood the time, one was the Farcroft in Rookery Rd, even though it was a tad smarter than some, and during the 40's and 50's it was the place to go for ballroom dancing, but it closed its doors in 1957 when teenagers wanted something different. Today we would say it didn't react quickly enough. It was still used for organised dances, but was never to be a threat to the Plaza just up the road.

To those of us who came from Winson Green and Handsworth, it was the nearest and best place to be, even though I've mentioned others they all needed a bus ride to get to them, and why travel when the best was on the doorstep? We did travel though, as variety is the choice of life. The West End was a second favourite with Margaret and myself. Sad to say this particular venue was to close owing to the rebuilding of Birmingham city centre (what a waste). We went dancing on a Monday to the Thimblemill Baths, when the wrestling wasn't on. But that's enough of me, it's the likes of Shiela Bolter from out of Talbot St who remembers when it was great to get dressed up on a Saturday night and go out with her friends to The Ninevah, Hawley's or the Tower. They would go in a gang but would relish the thought of being walked home by a 'fella'. Also Pattie Dimmock from up the Green who would have used all of these places, with, might I add, very fond memories, for all, I hope will read this book. The bands were real, no disco's, no live Karaoke in pubs, just plain dancing, and whatever else was to take it's course when it was time to go home!

Sheila Clemens and friend on a night out
(D Avery)

Girls night out at a firms dance - Margaret far left)
(Author's)

NEW CLOTHES AT EASTER

Whilst were still in this part of the Park and Lodge Road area, we can't forget Abbey and Goode Streets. I remember this part very well when I used to work for Scribbans' Bakery which was based in Goode St. It was a very busy street for most of the day as there were always vans and vehicles of all sorts going in and out the bakery, and anyone who was lucky to run a car in the street never stood much of a chance in parking it outside their house. There was one house in particular, right opposite the main entrance, this particular resident painted 'no parking' signs on the pavement. There was always a daily row between the resident and delivery men in parking their vans at this particular spot. Later on in the eighties when the bakery finally closed its doors, it would have been too late to complain, as most of the old properties had been knocked down or in the act of demolition, and if I remember rightly when I went to have a look around the area after the bakery and houses had been pulled down, the fading painted signs were still visible on the pavement.

Janice Bissel was born in Abbey St in 1947. She and her two brothers lived in that street for 12 years, and went to All Saints school, before the family moved to Handsworth. Her memories are so familiar to all of those who lived in this part, the trips to the 'Flat' for shopping on a Saturday, on a Friday her dad would walk up from there with a bag of delicious dripping cakes from Hunts, they would have these with a cup of tea before going shopping to Linleys in Lodge Rd for their groceries, dad would come as well as he would have to carry the shopping home in a cardboard box.

Having new clothes from Nortons at Easter at the bottom of Key Hill she remembers so well, her mother was very superstitious, and would always buy them at this time of the year. Later on they then moved to Handsworth. It was like another world, a bathroom with hot and cold running water, an inside lavatory, it seemed like a million miles away from the old days, when Janice and her brothers were to have their baths in front of the fire in the proverbial tin bath, whilst listening to Friday Night is Music Night on the wireless.

Living in Handsworth Janice goes to St Andrews Church, and there she met Mrs Ethel Dawes. She lived in Park Rd and told Janice of her time in

81

living in the area from 1943 to 1973. They lived at the back of Chillingsworth's grocery shop. Her husband worked on the railway, they had six children, three of them went to Benson Rd and the other three attended All Saints schools, Ethel was remembered as being a Guide Captain at All Saints. Ethels memories are still very much with her and recalls Mrs Kelly's grocery shop on the corner of Park Rd and Goode St and the red stone floor, and of the lady who lived at the back of the shop that used to wait for her husband to come home from work. She always wore a snow-white crossover apron. Ethel used to take the accumulators to Russells to be charged, and opposite Goode St was a little grocers who used to open on a Sunday. The owner would charge extra for goods on this day, her excuse was that if she got caught by the police it would help to pay the fine!

Though there were shops of all descriptions on the 'Flat' for selling clothes there were others as such as Dora Gray's in Park Rd. This was a house in which the upstairs doubled as a changing room for fittings, and of Miss Timms who made skirts for the Guides from her house.

On the corner of Orford St was a second hand shop, this was Bibby's. Mr Bibby used to play the fiddle in the street. All of these stones could be recounted by the number of people that gave me untold and wonderful information, no more so than Ethel who bought fireworks from Smith's the paper shop, but another Smith she didn't like was the one who kept a sweet shop at the bottom of Abbey St. He was a miserable sort of man, who always wore a flat cap and and what stood out in her memory was the watch and chain which adorned his waistcoat pockets. The sweets in the shop were always kept in small dishes in the window, and it was here that she first remembers Merry Maid chocolate caramels. Next door to Smith's was Silver's coalyard, then came Gilbert and Lloyds. This revived memories of Ethel of a Mrs Roper who lived close by, and the tragic accident in which her three babies were all burnt in a fire.

An unusual name for a shop was the 'Hole in the Wall'. It was a wine shop, run for a long time by Joan Grainger, a friend of Janice's mother. Janice and Ethel could go on about the shops and the area for ever and a day. Talking produces memories and others produce those same memories, sometimes in different circumstances.

We'll move away from Ethel and Janice and make our way finally to the shopping centre *par excellence* the 'Flat'.

Nortons on the corner of Icknield St and Key Hill
(J Landon)

AT LAST, THE FLAT

Shock of horrors, To find out that Tynegates wood yard was part of another area, and to find out that Winson Green only came as far as the 'cut' was cruel, didn't anybody think to tell us youngsters that our 'Flat' was also somebody else's back yard. The cruel reality of it all was that our mom hadn't told me. All this is tongue in cheek and we can now reflect, like I was once informed by a mate that Dudley Rd Hospital was in Brookfields, and not the Green. That was really rubbing salt into the wounds. Anyway I still regarded the 'Flat' as an extension to my little world. After the bus had struggled up and over the brow of the hill, another vista came into view, the tower of Scribbans' bakery, the Great Western railway goods yard and the long steep hill down to the 'Flat'

We were now in Brookfields. Touched by Hockley and Ladywood, and of course by Winson Green. Houses nestling side by side with shops, factories, pubs and the vast railway yard. It wasn't my area, and as far as I was concerned it was then just another part of our journey into the town, but it contained its own identity and to the people who lived in this small district who had their own tales to tell. But let's get back to the story. On the brow of the hill the canal made a perfect boundary, on the left hand side, lay the Ford Development Centre. Opposite on the other side of the road was the old fever hospital. Over the bridge was Tynegates wood yard and on the other side of the road was the British Oxygen works. This was a huge factory which ran down half of the remainder of Lodge Rd to Harmer St. The last remaining road was Paxton Rd with one solitary shop and of course it was to be a grocers, a double fronted shop ran by R and M Glews. (This was the only shop on the right hand side of Lodge Rd between Winson Green Rd and the 'Flat'!) We ask why a general store close to a main shopping centre? the same answer really of a small grocer close to the Merry Hill Shopping Centre. Well we all like somewhere convenient at the odd times! On the left hand side were terraced houses with small front gardens, then down to the railway bridge and Abbey Rd, next was Goode St and the smell of fresh baked bread emanating from Scribbans'. Then the bus pulled up outside the Hydraulic pub, a favourite watering hole for me and fellow bakery workers, or the Abbey public house across the road. Looking at the hill today it seems a short slope to how I remember it well. Houses ran down both sides of the hill, on the left

British Oxygen - 26 Oct 1961
(J Landon)

though was another pub, the Crown and Anchor, another M and B pub and yet further back houses behind this establishment, a bit further on down was Irene's Hair Fashions, houses took over the remaining buildings till Park Rd was met, and an Atkinsons public house occupied the corner. On the other side of the road coming down from the Hydraulic pub was mostly houses. When our old doctor died his patients were transferred to a new address. Gone were the terse days of Dr Mckeirnan, the practice was taken over by two brothers, one whom I remember had a rather large ginger beard. It was a relief to have a consultation lasting more than thirty seconds! though I take nothing away from McKeirnan as he was a fine and good doctor. Later the practice would move again to Hunters Rd, and to a Health Centre, but that was after my time. Houses still occupied the road till right at the bottom was a couple of factories, one was Charles Harris Ltd which was an engineers, it produced all sorts of tooling and metal pressings, and occupied four terraced houses which were converted into a factory, and next door was E W and F Twist.

This was now the 'Flat'. To the right Piddock St and off at an angle the remainder of Park Rd which ran down to Icknield St. Halfway along the 'Flat' on the left hand side was Heaton St.

We had arrived, now the shopping was about to be done in earnest.

This little shopping area will always be in our fondest memories. After Ford St shops such as Wine Shops Ltd proved that not everybody drank beer, then came Playfairs the shoe shop, lower down came Harry Spencers the greengrocers, flanked on one side by Myttons the butchers and the other one of Harry Spencers other trade, a poulterers, a wet fish shop and rabbit shop (Oh! the taste of rabbit stew from a long gone age). At Christmas time there would be Fir trees put up over the shutters to the shop, holly and mistletoe would be strung up, out would come the nuts, dates and tangerines, birds would be strung at his other shop. To name all of the shops in this small, but very busy area, would be a monologue, so I will pick some of the main ones out. Owing to the popularity of the area there were many of the big names side by side with their smaller cousins. Close to the corner of Heaton St was Scrivens the opticians, lower down was another butchers by the name of Burleys, after that was Joseph Harris the cleaners, then my favourite, George Masons, the grocers, the smell of smoked bacon, loose tea, blocks of cheese and butter, stands the test of time even to this day. (It wasn't on its own, the likes of Wrensons, Pearkes and Liptons spring to mind) Connie Timms was the manageress and a guy called Cyril was there when I was a lad. Next door was Popes the boys and gents outfitters, then Glarry's Fashions (down the Bull Ring there is a Glarry's shop is it the same one, or the same family?) for the ladies, if curtain materials were required Alan's was next door followed by Freeman Hardy and Willis for shoes. We were now on the corner of Lodge Rd and Icknield St, where Pooles the house furnishers stood, it was established in 1884. In the 50's it must have been a fore runner to the present day stores in offering credit with no deposit!

Large and small shops were to make up this shopping area, but to keep things in order Lodge Rd Pentecostal Church, home to many a marriage, christening and Sunday school, Vic Jones, the local photographer, captured many a happy moment, was next Woolworths. If a shopping centre was big enough a Woolworth's was to be found. It was as if an area had made it, and it complemented the other shops in the road. Small shops made their way up from Icknield St till another of Birmingham's favourite bakers, Wimbush's was to be found next to Woolworth's, after this came the Gas Service Showrooms followed by yet another small grocers W E Mapp's and next door a chemists, up the road was the Milk Bar a proper coffee house, used by all, including teenagers listening to the inevitable juke box, then another butchers, W A Clements. Next door was Sport and Play the bike shop, we were now coming to the end of this side of the 'Flat' and just before Piddock St was Yarnold's a large millinery shop.

Ford Works, previously a glass works dating from the 1700s
(J Landon)

I realise and apologise that I have missed out on quite a few shops, but I hope the reader will fill in the gaps with their own memory. The 'Flat' itself stretched a few hundred yards or more but what a shopping centre, over the years the old streets were to change, old property was pulled down and new housing was built, a lot of the shops were to close and never to reopen up again, names that were to be lost forever, even the day to day names were to disappear in the coming years. Even though today it still retains an area for shopping, of a kind, but there was never to be another 'Flat' as we knew it.

The memories of this part of our area will always live on, and those of us who returned time and time again to do their shopping , either as a grown up, or like me with our mom and aunts.

Before we leave the 'Flat', there is one hill that we should visit, that is Key Hill. The continuation of the 'Flat' was more shops, but it was one area I didn't know much about. There was one shop we all remembered and it was Norton's, which was on the corner of Key Hill and Icknield St. A large emporium for all which ran quite a way up the hill. More shops were to follow till it came to Great Hampton St. At the bottom on the other side of Key Hill was the Bulls Head an Ansells house. (If a beer drinker, we were now coming into Ansells territory, but back up our end M and B's were still in control.)

We've seen it, done it and wore the teeshirt, we've remembered the 'Flat', and what an important part it played in some of our lives. It's vibrancy, alive with it's shops and characters. I and thousands more were glad to have known and to have been in some little way a part of it.

Thank you 'Flat'

Looking up the Flat from Icknield St end
(J Landon)

*The Hydraulic. A watering hole for bakery workers and
the start of the long walk down to the Flat
(J Landon)*

*Tynegates Wood Yard, the canal bridge to the left of photo
(J Landon)*

Looking back up the 'Flat' on the left hand side
(J Landon)

The 'Flat'. It must have been early in morning as Christmas Decorations were
all out over the green grocers

90

The 'Flat' meeting Icknield St
(J Landon)

Our old shop - George Masons
(J Landon)

CONCLUSION

That's it. I've done as they say, the rounds. I started off with my little patch in Eva Rd. I've been up the Green to the Dudley Rd and all the way down to the 'Flat'. I've been to most of the pubs and visited lots of the shops along the way. I never knew them as such, but I shan't forget their names, We've visited the prison, we know where James Turner St got its name from, even my road was named after one of the two nurses who went with Florence Nightingale to the Crimea War. We've found something out about Guest, Keen and Nettlefolds and where Ivor Havins worked, about Pattie Dimmock and Jim Wilson from out of Heath St. About the Dolman Family and their house, the oldest property remaining on the Green, about Ted Rudge and Sheila Avery from the Lodge Rd area at the bottom end. Hilda Thomas who taught hundreds upon hundreds of children at Foundry Rd, and of others like Benson Rd, other schools and many places of worship. Our history and the make up of the area. The 32 tram preceding the 96 bus. The number 11 to other places in our city. The canals and railways which were to be a part of our growing up. The way to the 'Flat', going past the mental and fever hospitals, all now a memory I'm sorry to say. This in my youth was a vibrant area, and yet a friendly one. I've been fortunate, I've met a great many friendly folk along the way, and the willingness to help me put these books together. All of us though have helped in creating some sort of a lasting memorial to our small, but important part of this city. The Green isn't finished, it's still there, and will always be so. But our memories are of another time, of coal fires, outside lavatories and 'Miskins'. Buses and trams for local transport, the Midland Red as well as trains and 'Charra's' for holidays or days out. The Lickeys at Rednal and the Bluebell Woods down Hampstead Rd, these are my memories and to others from our district, and let's not forget 'The Black Patch' home to gypsies even before the prison was built. We are all part of the patchwork quilt that made our town into a city, Thank you Winson Green in letting me be a part of it.

For the Best Quality COOKED MEATS — kept under hygienic conditions in our modern fridge.

D. COOPER

242 WINSON GREEN ROAD

Agents for GRANTS Cakes, Pastries and Bread. Meat Pasties a Speciality.

PROGRAMME

for JANUARY, 1958

WINSON GREEN PALACE

Winson Green Road, Birmingham

Props: Winson Green Picture Palace Ltd.
Man. & Licensee: A. W. Hall. Tel. NORthern 1790
Front Stalls 1/6. Rear Stalls 2/3. Balcony 2/6
Reduced Prices for Children when accompanied by an Adult.

Important:— Children are not admitted to this Cinema without parents when an (A) Cert. film is being shown.

Monday, Tuesday, Wednesday, Thursday, Friday
Continuous 5-30 p.m.
Saturday Continuous 3-45 p.m.
Sunday 3-50 p.m.

FOR ALL HOME DECORATING SUPPLIES

J. GREAVES & CO.

66 & 87 WINSON GREEN ROAD

Crown Wallpapers, Bergermaster & Dulux Paints Distempers, Brushes, Varnishes, etc.

FOR THE PRIMEST QUALITY HOME KILLED MEAT

E. F. POTTER

Your Local Family Butcher
168 WINSON GREEN ROAD
SATISFACTION ALWAYS !

Before going to the show, get your SWEETS, CHOCOLATES and CIGARETTES — from

F. HYDE

216 WINSON GREEN ROAD
ALL THE BEST BRANDS IN STOCK

PETROL AND OILS
LODGE GARAGE
Corner of Bacchus Rd. and Lodge Rd.
Phone NOR 1752
Repairs — Overhauls
Greasing — Spares
Accessories.   Paraffin

S. POWELL

Newsagents, Tobacconists, Confectioners
223 BACCHUS ROAD, WINSON GREEN
Phone: NOR 5973

Prompt and early delivery of all Morning and Evening papers, periodicals, etc.

Trafalgar Publicity, Birmingham 24.

Programme from Winson Green Palace

93

Telephone: NOR 8135

PLUMBING. Installation & Repairs of all descriptions

D. F. RUSSON

71 Benson Road, Winson Green, Birmingham 18

SINK UNITS INSTALLED from £15.

FIRST CLASS FOOTWEAR REPAIRS BY CRAFTSMEN

TROMAN'S

192 BACCHUS ROAD, WINSON GREEN

Crepe, Rubber and Solution Work a Speciality.

Thursday, January 2nd   Three Days
Guy Madison in
BEAST OF HOLLOW MOUNTAIN   Ⓐ
Also Joseph Cotten in
The Halliday Brand   Ⓒ

Sunday, January 5th   Walter Pidgeon
MEN OF THE FIGHTING LADYⒶ
Robert Taylor in Valley of Kings   Ⓒ

Monday, January 6th   Three Days
Eddie Albert and Jack Palance in
ATTACK   Ⓐ

Joseph Cotten in
The Killer is Loose   Ⓐ

Thursday, January 9th   Three Days
Jack Lemmon and Ernie Novacs in
OPERATION MAD BALL   Ⓤ
Rory Calhoun in Domino Kid   Ⓤ

Sunday, Jan. 12th For FOUR Days
Barry Sullivan in
FORTY GUNS   Ⓐ
Also Heli on Devil's Island   Ⓤ

Thursday, January 16th   Three Days
Gary Cooper and Dorothy McGuire
FRIENDLY PERSUASION   Ⓤ

Sunday, January 19th
WATCH PRESS

Monday, January 20th   Three Days
Victor Mature and Diana Dors in
THE LONG HAUL   Ⓐ
Don Taylor and Sally Forrest in
Ride the High Iron   Ⓐ

Thursday, January 23rd   Three Days
WATCH PRESS

Monday, January 27th   Three Days
John Wayne and Maureen O'Hara in
WINGS OF EAGLES   Ⓒ
John Cassavetes, Sidney Poitier in
A Man is Ten Feet Tall   Ⓐ

Thursday, January 30th   Three Days
Hardy Kruger in
THE ONE THAT GOT AWAY   Ⓒ
Also The Naked Dawn   Ⓐ

RACING — FOOTBALL — GREYHOUNDS

JIM SMITH

COMMISSION AGENT
(Member B.P.A.)

57 CITY ROAD, EDGBASTON

ANTE POST BOOKS OPEN ON ALL
PRINCIPAL RACES

DAILY ACCOUNTS

Telephones :

EDG 2837   EDG 1335   NOR 4139

Programme from Regal Cinema, Handsworth

94

The Tower.

The Magazine of Bishop Latimer Memorial Church,
Birmingham, 18.

Published on the last Tuesday of each month for the succeeding month.

November, 1954.

3d. Monthly
By Post 4½

Bishop Latimers, Handsworth New Road

95